On the Shoulders of
GIANTS

On the Shoulders of
GIANTS

**LESSONS LEARNED FROM 25 YEARS OF BUSINESS
DEVELOPMENT THAT TRANSFORMED AN INDUSTRY**

JACK TESTER
CEO OF **NEXSTAR NETWORK**

The story of Frank Blau Jr.'s life that appears in the epilogue of this book was excerpted and adapted from the book *Soaring with Eagles: The Life and Legacy of Frank J. Blau Jr.* by Ellen Rohr and Helena Bouchez, published in partnership with Nexstar Network, Inc., St. Paul, Minnesota, 2016.

Jack Tester / Nexstar Network, Inc.
101 East 5th Street
St. Paul, Minnesota 55101
www.nexstarnetwork.com
info@nexstarnetwork.com

Editor: Candice Fehrman
Book design: Lori S Malkin Design, LLC

On the Shoulders of Giants / Jack Tester—1st ed.
ISBN 978-0-9992159-0-6

THIS BOOK IS DEDICATED TO:

*Frank Blau Jr., the founder of Nexstar and
the individual who started a transformation of this industry
that continues today. An individual who told you what you needed
to hear whether you wanted to listen or not. Thank you, Frank,
for giving this industry "the medicine."*

*Each member who cared enough to open their doors and
share their successes and failures with other members who were
relative strangers, who gave without asking and ultimately
discovered that they received far more than they gave.*

*Nexstar's dedicated staff, for embracing Frank's vision
and working tirelessly each day to bring it closer to reality—
you are extraordinary.*

———■———

If I have seen further, it is by standing on the shoulders of giants.
—ISAAC NEWTON

CONTENTS

FOREWORD

This is not just an excellent book and a great read, it is also a testament to you—the professional service provider.

This book will make you feel great about your profession. It will make you see that you are not just a WXYZ trade contractor—you are the owner of a professional service enterprise!

You make such a huge difference in our world. You improve people's lives—your customers, your employees, their families, and your own. In fact, you improve the entire community you serve.

You provide safety, health, comfort, energy efficiency, and so much more. You return conditions to normal when emergencies arise. And you are there whenever your customer wants and needs you to be. You actually do make dreams come true (plus remedy many nightmares).

You provide great value for a great service. And your career can be as rewarding and lucrative, with the highest of ethical standards, as any other professional practice. An honest day's pay, or I should say earning a very handsome income for an honest day's work, are not mutually exclusive—they are inextricably intertwined.

The key word in everything I have stated above is *you*, because this book is entirely about you and your profession. Read it, absorb it, learn from the lessons of the giants before you, and live the life you deserve.

With the greatest respect and admiration for what you do,

—**GREG NIEMI**,
FORMER PRESIDENT AND CEO, NEXSTAR NETWORK, 2001–2011

P.S. Someday, when the time is right for you, it will be your turn to give back to those who follow in your footsteps. Together we can make this world, including our profession, a better place.

P.P.S. Congratulations to all of Nexstar on your 25th anniversary. You are all life changers. I am so proud of all of you within the Nexstar Network, including our founders, members, board members, former members, retired members, staff, alumni, strategic partners, foundation trustees, speakers, trainers, volunteers, and so many more who have contributed your unique talents. ∎

WHY THIS BOOK

As I reflect on Nexstar's 25th year, I can't help but marvel at the changes in the plumbing, heating, cooling, and electrical (PHCE) contracting industry, especially the evolution of its service and replacement sector. And I'm incredibly proud of Nexstar's role in accelerating that evolution.

I'm also proud of *our* evolution as an organization—especially our ability to capitalize on our successes and learn and grow from our missteps.

Over the past 25 years, Nexstar has amassed an amazing depth of PHCE business-specific knowledge along with a deep understanding of the key success factors required to create a thriving PHCE service and replacement business.

But if we've learned anything over the past two and a half decades, it's that success in the service and replacement business is in the *nuances* and *details*. Generalized business advice can take the PHCE service business owner just so far. To make it the rest of the way, owners need very specific advice that accounts for those nuances and details and how they get translated into success.

Nexstar and its members have been extraordinary at homing in on those nuances and details, along with a host of other factors required for success for every role in the company, from the owner to the apprentice technician— everything that makes each function in the business *extraordinary*. Because being extraordinary is what creates success.

From day one, Nexstar's mission has been to provide everything the service contractor needs to succeed. Our coaches and trainers today are skilled and knowledgeable in the specifics of this industry, and our online libraries are stuffed with operational processes, training videos, and lessons—everything you could possibly need to grow a profitable service and replacement company.

As we approached our 25th year, however, it hit me that there was no one place where Nexstar's overall philosophy and approach was articulated, nothing that outlined for the next generation all that Nexstar has learned specifically for the benefit of the owner of a PHCE business.

This book aims to change that.

For the first time, the essence of Nexstar's philosophy and thinking is available all in one place. In the pages of this book, you will find the success principles and mind-sets that owners, senior leaders, and leadership teams need to have as the business scales up, every step of the way.

Making Nexstar's approach and point of view more widely available to *all* contractors allows more people to stand on our shoulders to see what's possible, inspiring them to reach higher and do better. Current and past members of Nexstar may experience this book as a refresher course on lessons already learned (and perhaps forgotten) or find that it rekindles some enthusiasm!

The mission of this book is to support you, the hardworking PHCE business leader, in your goal to create a thriving contracting business—one that will allow you to create a great life for you and your employees and live the way you truly want and deserve to live. Because creating a great life is what this book—and Nexstar—is all about.

I sincerely hope you enjoy the book. Even more so, I hope it will inspire you to begin changing your business into one that will allow you to enjoy your life more both now and in the years to come.

—JACK TESTER,

PRESIDENT AND CEO, NEXSTAR NETWORK, AUGUST 2017

HOW DO YOU WANT TO LIVE?

The typical plumbing, heating, cooling, and electrical (PHCE) company that joined Nexstar in 1992 looked exactly like the industry at the time—small, with fewer than six employees, family run, and strong technically, but lacking in business acumen and professionalism. Total annual sales of the average new member were less than $1 million annually, and much of this was still in new construction.

Today, the average Nexstar member performs $6 million of service and replacement business annually and does so with very little new construction work. In fact, we have many members doing north of $30 million in service replacement sales from a single location, a sum unfathomable in 1992.

Over the last 25 years, we have witnessed hundreds of businesses grow from struggling dysfunctional family affairs to highly profitable business powerhouses providing amazing careers to thousands of employees. And in the process, we have helped drive a positive transformation in this industry.

Nexstar was founded to be the "nexus" or link in this industry's transformation, but we have also had the privilege of growing and learning right along with it. How many organizations can say they have had that opportunity to learn both the success factors of growing a very small business and a very large one? None that we know of. We learned these success factors through hard work, sharing successes, and building on the work of industry giants who came before us.

The title of this book, *On the Shoulders of Giants*, is a phrase with special meaning to us at Nexstar. By standing on the shoulders of those who came before us, we gain a vantage point unavailable to us alone. We learn from the giants' experiences and get better opportunities because of the wisdom we acquire from them.

Nexstar was founded on the core value of "success through education and sharing."

It is our hope that the stories and success principles in this book provide you with a unique window into your own potential, so you too can eventually become a giant. The purpose of this book is to help you get what you really wanted when you decided to go into business—a thriving PHCE service business that would allow you and your employees to live the way you all really want to live.

Not how your friends think you should be living. Not how general contractors or home warranty companies think you should be living. And certainly not how your worst, cheapest competitors think you should be living. How *you* want to live.

We want to reconnect you, the owner, with the grand vision you had when you jumped into business—a vision of money, freedom, and accomplishment.

Amid the daily grind of starting and running a business you may have lost sight of that vision. This book is going to take you back to it. And if you read it all the way through and put into practice the principles that are laid out, you will find success.

When it comes to how you want to live, we want you to know you have a choice. And the mission of this book is to bring that choice to light and give you the courage to embrace it and turn it into reality.

Why?

Because you are worth it.

■ You Are Worth It

Nexstar Network Founder Frank J. Blau Jr.[1] once said, "If you elect to go into business, and you are doing something to better society, you deserve to do well."

I've known Frank a long time, so let me tell you when he said "do well" he did not mean just survive and pay the bills. He meant *thrive* in every

---

[1] A summary of Frank's fascinating life story appears at the end of this book.

sense of the word. He meant be able to take care of your family and have the time and resources to pursue hobbies and philanthropic interests. That is what Frank meant by do well, and that is what I mean too.

You deserve to thrive as a small-business owner—*especially* as a PHCE business owner.

A big part of Frank's life mission was to help honest, hardworking people become extraordinary at what they do so they could thrive like he did. At Nexstar, we also believe that if you do great work, you deserve to live well and thrive, even if you only have one truck.

We believe that you deserve to create and grow a business that will enable you to live an amazing life rather than letting other people determine the kind of life you should lead or limit you because of their own low self-esteem or flawed belief systems.

Because when a business is doing great, and the owner is thriving, there's an opportunity for the employees in that company to do great and thrive too. And as part of that process, customers are taken care of and the industry and community at large is enhanced as well.

A well-run small business is like a rising tide—it lifts *all* boats.

PROTECTING THE PUBLIC

If you're like most contractors, you probably don't see the true value of what you do. To you, the work is something you do every day with relative ease and you don't realize how truly special you are.

For example, every PHCE company we know has prevented serious harm and even death for customers. Sure, most days will be routine, fixing a flapper on a toilet, installing an outlet, or installing an outside AC unit. But those days are routine only because the work is done correctly. Remember that. Most days are routine only because *you are amazing.* That same task in the hands of a novice could be damaging and potentially deadly!

And what about the times you discovered the presence of toxic carbon monoxide or noxious sewer gas that an elderly customer could not smell? Or spotted a faulty electrical panel that was just waiting to start a fire? Or repaired a frozen pipe that was ready to flood a house?

If you think about all you have prevented, the property and lives you have saved and enhanced—can you really charge too much?

I'm asking you to step back and think about the contribution your trade makes to the quality of people's lives and feel great about that so you can stop giving it all away.

Think about this: McDonald's contribution to society is that it offers consistently bad fast food anywhere in the world. That isn't a contribution to mankind; it's a crime. Yet McDonald's makes around 20 percent net profit for its contribution. Looked at this way, who deserves the higher profit percentage—McDonald's or you, a hardworking contractor?

To that end, Apple makes a 38 percent net profit, yet no one calls them crooks or accuses them of ripping off the public because they charge $800 for a phone. Can you imagine Apple making a decision to drop its prices because its profits are too high and therefore unethical? No way.

By the way, Apple's competitors are thrilled the iPhone is that expensive because it resets expectations and means they can raise their prices too. I wish our industry thought the same way!

The leader of Apple is not called a crook by his own industry and he doesn't feel bad about the cost of the phone either. Neither do Apple's employees or its shareholders. Think about all of this the next time you run into a customer or colleague who says you are too expensive. Are you worth more than a phone or a hamburger? We think so.

You are worth it, and if you're willing to work hard to get even better, you should be charging a lot—look at what you do!

CREATING NOBLE, HONORABLE JOBS

The amazing service you provide to customers is not the only reason you deserve to be highly paid. The other reason is you're creating honorable jobs that aren't going to be outsourced or done in a radically different way anytime soon.

The jobs well-run PHCE companies create are highly valued field, office, and management positions. They aren't just jobs; they are lifelong careers. They also are not the short-term, highly volatile jobs created in high-tech companies that are here today and shipped overseas tomorrow.

These positions are staffed by people with lifelong skills that they will always be able to use wherever they may be. A highly trained service technician can get a job in any town in America. There are not many professions that can make that claim.

Small business is the backbone of America. The sense of pride, community, and connection you feel as an owner of a successful local business cannot be overstated.

But even if you weren't out there ensuring public safety or doing service calls at 1:00 a.m. on a subzero night, the fact that you are out there creating good, honorable jobs and contributing to your community makes you deserving of high pay. Thank you and congratulations!

NOT GOOD ENOUGH FOR A REAL PROFESSION

For many of us, unless you grew up in a family business, going into the trades probably wasn't your first choice. People land in the trades for any number of reasons. Maybe you grew up in a blue collar neighborhood where being a tradesman was almost expected of you. Maybe you weren't the kind of student who guidance counselors pointed toward college. Maybe you are great with your hands but bad at learning in a typical classroom environment. Or maybe you are dyslexic or have ADHD. Many people settle for a job in the trades to pay the bills until something better comes along. Learning a trade provides you with an opportunity to acquire a valuable skill set that enables you to make a living.

This also might explain why the trades tend to be filled with people with low self-esteem. Even after people get their license and go on to start a business, so many still lack a sense of self-worth.

If you're like many contractors we know, the story you are stuck with is, "I'm not good at school and not good at numbers," and so you avoid further classroom instruction and anything that has to do with math. That's understandable. Who wants to feel ridiculed and stupid?

The problem is that avoiding these things almost guarantees business underperformance and financial suffering.

Here's how it typically plays out for a new business owner. When you first start out you think, "I don't have any overhead, so to get the business started I'll just charge hourly rates that are less than my closest competitors."

The problem is you do have overhead—a truck, fuel, office supplies, tools, and more—none of which has been factored in. Your selling price is nearly guaranteed to be too low to allow you to break even, much less live the way you want to live!

But to most newly minted business owners who are scrambling to get a business going, being the lowest-priced provider seems like the most logical thing to do. After all, no one hangs out a shingle with the goal of being more expensive. Except that is exactly what we did when 16 brave contractors joined together to start Nexstar (then called Contractors 2000) in 1992.

At the time, the typical trade association dues were less than $500 per year. These organizations had been in existence for decades. Five hundred dollars was the going rate for contractor organizations.

With a traditional start-up mind-set, you would think we would have set dues around $400—just a little bit lower than the competition so we could get the work.

Instead, that first year, before we had delivered even one member benefit, we set dues at $4,000. We had no desire to be competitively priced because we knew what we were worth and what it would cost to deliver value for our members. In that first year, if we had decided to be "competitive," we would have been out of business within two years.

Instead, we decided to charge $4,000 because we wanted to deliver extraordinary value to our members. That's right; we didn't have anything to offer yet and we still thought we were worth it! We consciously decided not to compete with other associations that did not provide the value to members that we were planning to provide.

It wasn't easy. Many contractors balked at our prices and decided we were too expensive. We took a lot of heat. We were laughed at and derided by many in the industry.

FAKE COUGH IN CLEVELAND

One incident I remember vividly. It was in our first year of operation. I was presenting the benefits and the different plans of Nexstar to a group of contractors in Cleveland, Ohio. When I stated the price of membership, one contractor very deliberately started to loudly and dramatically fake cough and said, "You gotta be kidding me!"

This was not a one-on-one conversation. This was in front of 50 fellow contractors! He was so self-righteous, smug, and proud of his taunting.

No one enjoys being laughed at in public. I am sure my face was beet red. But still I believed in what we were doing and what we were charging. While embarrassing, it also provided me with even more motivation to succeed, to prove to this industry and people like this self-righteous contractor that we would make something special out of Nexstar. I think about this individual from time to time and wonder how the going rate has treated him.

As for Nexstar, at the time of this writing—almost 25 years later—we have 560 active members performing more than $3 billion in service and replacement revenue. The typical Nexstar member's business is growing internally at more than 10 percent and has annual profits in excess of 10 percent.

We work and train in a beautiful high-rise office building in St. Paul, Minnesota, and have a professional staff of 45 dedicated individuals who are helping thousands of people improve their lives and build amazing careers. If we had let the Cleveland incident shame us into dropping our price, we would have failed our members, our future employees, and this industry.

We deeply understood the principles that we're about to lay out for you in this book, so we knew that if we were to succeed we would need to walk our talk from day one. From day one we had to *be* the kind of organization we needed to be—from the way we acted to the prices we charged.

We were charging a lot, so members would have the right to expect a lot. We couldn't be average; we had to be extraordinary. And believe me, there was immense pressure to deliver.

And that's the deal. If *you* want to charge what you need to create a business that will provide a secure future for your family (and the people who will be working for you), you have to commit to being extraordinary too. You can't charge the right price and then act like the going rate. You have to be *better*.

The good news is that you can be extraordinary. It is really not that hard, and we're going to show you how. And we have 560 members who will testify that being extraordinary every day is well worth the effort.

YOUR BIGGEST OBSTACLE: YOU

There will be obstacles. But the biggest obstacle you will face in creating a business that will enable you to live the way you want to live has nothing to do with external circumstances such as your competitors or the economy—and everything to do with your current mind-set and beliefs.

The problem is not your intelligence or ability. It's that somewhere along the way you bought into some limiting beliefs about what you can and can't do, beliefs others foisted on you as a kid, which tanked your self-esteem.

The good news is that the path to success turns out to be a lot less about what's going on around you and much more about the will and wisdom inside you, the owner, to think differently about yourself and your business.

This news is good because while you can't do anything about your competitors or the economy, you can do a lot about your own will and wisdom. You can change the way you think about yourself and your work.

TAKING OUT THE HEAD TRASH

One of the bigger tasks you face is identifying and clearing out the "head trash" that is blocking your way to success. "Head trash" is a series of stories you tell yourself that reflect your mind-set and beliefs. Stories such as:

"I can't charge $400/hour; that's just greedy."
"I just want to stay small."
"I don't care about money."
"If I charge too much, I won't have any customers."
"I want to sleep at night."
"I don't want it."

By the way, in our experience "I don't want it" is code for "I don't think I can do it." Who would not want more money and comfort? Who *wants* to work their entire life for less than they could otherwise? Our question to you is this: How do you know you can't do it?

We're betting you can. Why? Because we've known hundreds of owners who have done it, including some who struggled so mightily in classrooms that they never graduated high school.

Making these mind-set shifts can be tough, but those who do it typically have had a moment of clarity when they decided they no longer were willing to let their low self-esteem and the opinions of others get in the way of living the way they wanted to live.

Admit it—wouldn't it be nice to be able to afford to do things now rather than waiting? For example, to be able to thoroughly train everyone in your company and pay them (and yourself) well rather than struggling at a subsistence level year after year under the self-delusion that somehow, someway things will get better—even though nothing is changing?

For too many contractors, "Next year!" becomes the rallying cry, but it's one that's voiced more softly and with less conviction with each passing year.

We urge you to stop all of that right now—just *stop!*

We believe that someone who gives great value to the world deserves to have a great business and that means you, too.

Are you ready to get out of your own way and create a business that delivers what you want and the means to live the way you want to live?

■ It's up to You

Years of experience helping contractors just like you has proved to us one thing: success is a matter of self-determination. It is a *personal choice*—not luck or fate!

In fact, if you just accept what the world gives you, I guarantee you will be disappointed. You, and only you, need to determine what you need and want in this life. So we invite you to decide how you want to live and then set your business up to deliver what you need to do just that.

You'll need to figure out how much money you and the business need to make to live the way you want to live—without being a slave to the business.

When you finally know that number, you can then begin charging the price that will enable you to achieve it.

Don't let anyone else tell you what you need to charge to get there! They don't know your goals, and you don't know if they are thriving in their own life enough to earn the right to give you advice. Nexstar Founder Frank Blau Jr. had a vehement disdain for "false prophets"—those who dared to profit from offering other contractors business advice when their own contracting businesses were flagging or even failing!

It would be wise for you to share the same disdain for other people's unsolicited, uninformed opinions about what you should be doing in your own life.

■ In This Book

This book is meant as an operating guide and source of inspiration, a "yes, I can" book for the nonbusiness person who has started a PHCE business and wants to learn more about how to grow it successfully. If you're tired of settling for a substandard existence or looking for a way out from having to work all the time for little pay or less profit, this book is for you.

We've broken the information into four sections: Apprentice, Journeyman, Master, and finally, Giant. The following is a snapshot of what's in each section.

APPRENTICE

In the apprentice section, you'll learn the foundational business principles behind every successful PHCE business. We start by addressing the question that every contractor faces—pricing.

You'll learn why your price has to be based on the way you want to live and not on what your competitors are charging or what you believe the market will bear.

More importantly, we'll explain what you'll face in defending that high price and why you need to make sure you're also delivering a high level of service to match.

We'll explain how customers really think about your service (hint: you are way too close to it!) and how you should think about the unavoidable conflict and criticism that comes with a price change.

You'll also learn why the only situation in which you can create the value required to charge enough is if you are selling directly to the person who is writing the check and will be personally experiencing your good work, and not to a third-party agent such as a general contractor, home warranty company, or off-site property manager.

You'll see why cash is king and learn why you should never leave a job without collecting payment for your services. And how your customers feel when the job is done is what matters most. Period.

We'll also challenge you to get out of the truck as soon as possible so you can spend your time working *on* your business instead of *in* it. This is a big hurdle for most contractors because it involves a change in day-to-day activities. You'll miss working with your hands, but you'll love the results of focusing on growing your business.

All these business fundamentals are important, but hiring great people (especially the very first employee) precedes everything in level of importance. We'll provide you with some guidance on selecting that first critical hire.

We'll also be showing you why you have to sell it before you can do it. We'll provide you with some insights to help you overcome your baggage around selling and some stories of how others have done it successfully.

And last but not least, we'll show you how you can not only make peace with your financials, but also fall in love with those numbers.

JOURNEYMAN

As a journeyman business owner, you have the fundamentals down and you're doing enough right that you can carve out a nice profit and focus on growing your business.

In this section, we'll explain the importance of keeping it simple and growing what you know. And how firming up your business processes can accelerate your growth and reduce the hassles of a larger, more complex business. We'll also cover how important it is to stay focused and not let yourself be unnecessarily distracted by what your competitors are doing. After all, you don't know if what they do is really working for them or if it is right for you!

We'll walk you through some basics of building and managing a high-performing team and making sure those who perform well for you can thrive.

You'll also learn why you need to set and meet daily goals, why you need to share those goals with employees, and how to contort the business to meet those goals every single day.

You'll learn the magic of an approach called "Be-Do-Have," and we'll invite you to aspire to more and surround yourself with people who are doing the same.

MASTER

At this level, you've achieved your financial goals and so creature comforts and financial security are no longer an issue. At the master level, it's no longer about what's in it for you; it's about your legacy and the contribution you want to make to society. We'll talk about how to sustain your passion and why, at this point, momentum matters more than ever.

We'll also talk about some of the success traps you may fall into, and how to avoid or extricate yourself from them. And why at this point you can leave your business for a couple of weeks for vacation, but you can't move and run your business from the beach without some big consequences.

You'll learn what you need to do as the owner to develop the leaders that will enable you to eventually pass on control of the business, and how to manage common conflicts that emerge when all companies grow to a certain size.

We will also help you understand that as the owner and custodian of this thriving business, you are never finished personally growing intellectually and emotionally, because the minute you do, your business will stop growing as well.

GIANT

The trades stop at master, but here at Nexstar there is one more level, and that is giant. At this level you're fully engaged in training your managers to think like you do so they can make decisions that are as good as (or better than) yours.

Those decisions create alignment with your vision so the company continues to grow and thrive.

However, it's when you've created a business full of amazing people who are *willing and able to pass on all they've learned to others* that you become a giant.

We'll provide you with a specific example of how this works, starting with Frank's mentoring of an early Nexstar member. We'll show you how sharing your knowledge with others can change not only their lives, but also the lives of those they go on to invite to stand on their shoulders and see new possibilities.

Naturally, we hope to inspire you all to become giants, but to get there, you first have to experience the journey yourself.

The first step is to learn what *you* need to do to live the way *you* want to live.

Ready? Great. Let's get started. ■

APPRENTICE

APPRENTICE

Now that you've dared to claim how it is you really want to live (because you're worth it), this first section is designed to help you understand what needs to change in your business so you can achieve that vision.

To that end, you'll learn about pricing and what your customers *really* think about your services and how much they should or shouldn't cost. (Hint: they're not thinking about it at all.) Then you'll be introduced to three rules that, if embraced, have the power to change your contracting business for the better on *day one*.

You'll also learn why you need to get out of the truck as soon as possible, the importance of getting the first hire right, and the right way to think about sales because—let's face it—you've got to sell it before you can do it.

Finally, you'll be encouraged to reframe the way you think about the numbers—in hopes that you'll fall as deeply in love with them as we have—along with so many other successful contractors who have made the shift.

If these concepts are new to you, you may feel a little overwhelmed. That's understandable and it's also OK. Put the book down, take a deep breath, and *keep going*. Then do what you can as soon as you can and watch your business start to change—today.

THE PRICE IS THE PRICE

■ Where Do Numbers Come From?

The first step toward living the way you really want to live is to stop and think about what you're charging.

Where did you get those numbers?

Are they based on a budget that reflects what it would really cost to live the way you want to live? Have you been realistic on all the overhead costs that you truly need to run a solid business? Have you accurately determined how many hours your company will need to sell to recover all of those costs? Or are they based on those destructive old saws, "what I think the market will bear" or "the going rate"?

Or worse, maybe you're asking prospective customers what it would take to get their business and then saying yes to whatever number they give without considering what your true costs are.

Here's the problem with all of this: what you need to charge for your services is a function of the expenses needed to meet your goals and live great—that's *reality*. What an individual customer offers to pay you for your services is not.

What if you engineered your life first? What if you got honest about what it is you really want, what you need to live greatly—including how much money you need to bring in to be able to pay yourself and your employees what you are all really worth?

Let that sink in.

Now, let's break it down.

Most service businesses don't sell anything unless labor hours are attached. That means to be successful you've got to come up with an hourly labor rate that is based in reality.

Let's be clear right here on mistakes most start-up contractors make. They overestimate how much time they can charge to customers and underestimate how much time they need to tend to other things in the business. These two mistakes, coupled with underestimating overhead expenses, create a real cash crunch and lead to the demise of most small businesses. Thinking about pricing in the right way can help keep this from happening.

GETTING TO THE RIGHT PRICE

If you work full time as a one-man shop, you have 2,000 work hours available to you annually. That gives you 40 hours a week with two weeks off for vacation.

Sure, you could work more hours, but is that why you started your own business? To work nonstop? Or was it to have a better life? So let's stay with 2,000 hours.

When you consider that much of your time will be buying inventory, returning calls, and working on marketing or other activities that you can't bill to a customer, at most you will be able to bill about 50 percent of that time, which is 1,000 hours. (Remember that number.)

Let's say you want to pay yourself $150,000 a year and you are a one-truck operator. In addition to that amount, you have a certain amount of overhead (i.e., office supplies, fuel, repairs, vehicle payments, tools, mobile phone, Internet, marketing, accountants, payroll taxes, etc.). Let's say all of this also adds up to $150,000 per year. To be able to cover $150,000 of overhead expenses and pay yourself $150,000 a year, you have to bring in $300,000 in revenue!

To get to the billing rate you really need, divide the revenue needed—$300,000—by how many hours you have to bill, which we've decided is 1,000: *$300,000 / 1,000 = $300*

That's right, in this scenario, to cover all your expenses, your billing rate would need to be $300/hour. And that is just to break even! No profit.

"But wait," you say, "I'm a one-truck operation and I'm getting paid my $150,000 a year. What do I need profit for?"

You might not need it personally, but if your business is to sustain itself and grow, it needs to create some profit dollars to do that.

Let's say you decide you are just as deserving of a 20 percent profit as McDonald's, so you add a 20 percent profit to your selling price. Here is the equation: *$300 / .80 = $375*

That's right. To make a 20 percent profit, your new billing rate will have to be $375/hour.

That's reality. That's the real world. Billing $375/hour for 1,000 hours a year, to achieve $375,000 in revenue, is what has to happen in order to cover your overhead, pay yourself, and create a profit equal to a hamburger stand.

When confronted with this reality, at this point you have three choices:

1 • You can decide that price is just too high, charge a lower price, and live on less than $150,000.

2 • You can work way more than 2,000 hours to create additional hours to bill. This means you will be working 10 or 12 hours a day, six or seven days a week.

3 • You can charge the correct price, work a manageable number of hours, and have the life you envisioned when you went into business.

It's a simple decision that is hugely important.

Your hourly rate has to be based on what you want to make, what you're really worth, and how you want to live. Period. Your selling price is not a function of other people's opinions—friends, family, coworkers, or customers. *Your selling price is up to you.*

Get your head around this idea—it is supremely important.

The example we have used is for a single-truck operation. But exactly the same concept applies as more field employees are added to the business. It all comes down to the right selling price based on the life you want to live and the company you want to create. There is no other reality.

Once you've validated your price through the budgeting process, the price is the price! Stick with it. This may be challenging at first, but hold your ground. Remember, you are worth it.

OVERHEAD: THE CUSTOMER PAYS FOR EVERYTHING

"The customer pays for everything because it's in their best interest to do so," said Frank Blau Jr. When Frank said everything, he meant *everything*, meaning all that it costs you to provide your customers with top-notch service.

Overhead, as it turns out, is not the enemy! And it is in your customers' best interest to help you pay for it *all*.

Think about it this way. If you don't charge the customer enough for your service, how can you afford to support a callback in a timely fashion? Not having to go back at all is in your and the customer's best interest, which means you need to spend money to thoroughly train your staff to make sure they know how to do the job correctly the first time.

Warranty calls, callbacks, staff trainings—all of these things translate to significant overhead expenses. How will you afford them unless you can fully fund them? And how will you do that unless you are charging what you need to charge?

Answer: unless you charge the right price, your overhead will leech away your profits and, eventually, your paycheck too.

STICKING TO IT (THE PRICE IS THE PRICE)

Sometimes sticking with and getting the new price will be easy and exciting. I remember talking to a longtime Nexstar member who had always operated under the tyranny of the going rate. He visited Frank's shop in 1991, and after he got home, he decided to give flat-rate pricing at a much higher hourly rate a try.

I remember him telling the story of the first call he ran with the new prices. It was a shower faucet repair. He looked at his new price, which was three times his old price. He then showed the price to the customer in his brand-new flat-rate book and the customer said yes—no questions asked. He was *stunned*. He said the day before he would have sold the job for one-third of that price and still thought it was on the high side of the market. He was a changed man. This call and this moment of clarity changed his life. He had been undervaluing what he had been doing for decades, but not anymore.

Other times, sticking to your price will be harder. Your customers, industry competitors, or even your friends—who don't understand your business or

Going Broke with the Going Rate
John Conway

Within my first year of membership at Nexstar, I started to learn how much it really cost to operate a service company. I had always believed and lived out in my business that the "customer is always right, even when they are wrong." This level of customer satisfaction doesn't come cheap. So armed with these facts, I decided that we were going to charge the prices that it cost to operate our company.

You see, the biggest myth in our industry is something called the "going rate." Have you ever heard of the going rate? You know, what's the going rate for Freon? What's the going rate for a 50-gallon water heater? What's the going rate for a three-ton condenser? We have all heard of the going rate or market price. Can I tell you something? The going rate usually equals going broke.

So who determines the going rate? I mean, let's just grab our phone and call him up! Um, you don't know his number. So let me get this right. We are going to determine selling price based on some myth that has absolutely nothing to do with what it costs to operate our company? We are going to base our future and the future of our family and our employees and their families based on this myth? We are going to base our ability to pay our vendors and cover our overhead on this myth? We are going to base our ability to produce a 25 percent net profit on this myth? I don't think so. We better know how much it costs to operate our company by the hour, by the day, by the week, month, and year. You are worth the fee!

> *"We have all heard of the going rate or market price. Can I tell you something? The going rate usually equals going broke."*

your goals—may try to shame you back into poverty by calling you a rip-off artist or worse! Don't let them influence you. Stick to your plan.

The bottom line is that you either need to charge enough or get out of business entirely, because no matter how hard you try you will not be able to outrun the numbers. They will catch up with you. They are the reality. The opinions of others are not.

You're not alone. Most small businesses (not just PHCE) don't have any idea what they need to charge! The problem with the typical small-business financial model is that it's destined to lose you money until one of two things happens: you learn a new way of looking at it and change your approach and your price, or you finally go out of business because "it's just too competitive out there." That doesn't serve anyone.

▣ Change Your Price, Change Yourself

When the selling price is low, you or your techs might feel justified in treating the customer badly, dressing poorly, working sloppy, or being late, because, after all, you're the "cheapest" guy. You might actually think you are doing the customer a *favor* by charging a low price.

The reality is you're not doing either of you any favors by aspiring to be the cheapest guy. But if you are going to charge the higher price, the deal is you have to match it with a higher level of service. You have to deliver at a higher level so you can feel good about that money.

This is a *huge* mind-set shift for most people—I know that. It simply has to happen. Charging the right price will enable you to create the right company and the right customer service experience. It is impossible to do this if you are charging the wrong price.

Maybe you plan to raise your prices someday when your service improves. I can't tell you how many times I have heard this. And in almost all cases "someday" never comes. This is faulty thinking.

Having a higher price immediately creates an incentive to deliver a better service experience. Charge the right price and then *become* the kind of company that deserves that price.

Remember when we started Nexstar? We had nothing to offer other than a promise, and we started charging 10 times the rate of typical contractor organizations. We could not say, "We will get better later." We had to *be* great now. Charging what we knew we were worth forced us to be extraordinary from day one. And you can do the same thing in your business by changing your pricing, but only if you're willing to become worthy of that pricing right away.

Frank Blau Jr. made a personal commitment to living how he wanted, and then figured out how to contort his business to deliver that rather than contorting his life to fit whatever was happening in the business. He charged the right price and made sure that the service delivered was worthy of that price.

Through his courses and columns and in the founding of Nexstar, Frank went on to mentor thousands of contractors in how to do what he did.

A mentor is someone who looks after you, who has been where you've been, and who can help you do those things they know from experience will create success. Someone whose shoulders you can stand on to see where you need to go and how to get there.

I invite you, through this book, to stand on our shoulders and catch a glimpse of what's really possible. You can do it, and *you are worth it.* ■

2

HOW CUSTOMERS THINK

L et's say you are a typical plumbing contractor and you install three water heaters a week for $1,100 each. You may think, "I can't charge more because that's all it is worth." You think that because you are conditioned to believe that is what a water heater is worth.

You deal with water heaters every day. You wake up thinking about water heaters and go to bed thinking about water heaters. You have had a customer or two tell you that $1,100 is the going rate for water heaters. And you have had others tell you that it's too expensive.

But is your premise accurate? How do you know?

■ You Are Too Close to It

Let's think about your typical customer for a moment. Unlike you, your customer doesn't think about water heaters until they need one. For the most part, your work is the furthest thing from their mind. Most homeowners buy maybe two water heaters in their entire life, and these typically are not planned purchases that are extensively researched in the same way a new deck or a fishing boat is researched.

Sure, a few customers with time on their hands will do this, but just a few. So when the water heater goes out, the customer calls around to find someone who can replace it. If the person on the other end of the line is nice; if the technician shows up on time, treats the customer with respect, leaves the area clean, and does good work; and if the price is $1,800, what we've have found again and again is that few customers will think twice about paying that amount. They are not "calibrated" to a price of $1,100 for a water heater like you are. They're just happy the experience was good and that it's done. They move on with life and put you and water heaters out of their mind.

For example, I don't know what a water heater costs or should retail for from a reputable contractor and *I am in this business*! I have a range in my head, mostly because I bought a new water heater for my house just last year. Even so, I don't remember exactly what I paid. Somewhere between $1,500 and $2,000, I think. The point is, I'm still not sure, even though this is my business and I just bought one. The typical customer has little or no frame of reference whatsoever. They just know they want hot water!

We use water heaters as an example, but the same is true of electrical and heating-cooling services. Consumers don't think about our trades until they need us.

What customers are looking for is someone they trust to give them a fair value. How they determine that is based on two things: the trust you build up when presenting them with options and how they feel at the end of the job.

Pricing problems occur when customers sense a high price coupled with low professionalism or shoddy workmanship. Then their antennas perk up and you have a price complaint.

Pricing has less (much less) to do with customer expectations and the "market price" and a whole lot more to do with recognizing and evicting the "head trash" that resides between your ears about what you should be charging.

■ Criticism Will Happen (Just Make It Worth the Fight)

Criticism and price complaints will happen, so don't be crestfallen and retreat to the going rate when they occur. Know that not everyone is going to agree with you. Accept that there is going to be this new conflict in your life when you start to sell at the right price. If you're currently not charging enough, you've already got conflict in the form of not having enough money to pay bills or meet goals and live the life you truly deserve. And even at that selling price I'm betting you *still have price complaints*!

Wouldn't you rather have the conflict that comes with charging the right price than the conflict that comes with the consequences of charging the going rate? Put it this way: Would you rather deal with bill collectors or deal with having to defend your price to a few complainers?

You are always going to have conflict in your business. Why not make it to your benefit?

You're also going to work your eight hours a day either way. Let's figure out how to pay you the most for those eight hours.

Coming to terms with the fact that you will have conflict in your business whether you charge the right price or the going rate is huge. There is no coasting through life with customers forever smiling and agreeing with your every move. There always will be some criticism and complaining to deal with as long as you're in business.

The key is to opt to receive the kind of criticism and complaints that occur because you are consciously creating a company that will allow you to live the way you really want to live. ■

The Wrong Price

John Conway

I bought a struggling HVAC new-construction company from my father in 1998. At that time the business had previous year's revenues of $2.1 million—$2 million in new construction and $100,000 in service and replacement.

I had always heard the money to be made was in the service industry rather than new construction, and specifically in flat-rate pricing. So within one month of purchasing the business, I called a flat-rate company to purchase a book.

The gentleman at the flat-rate company, Andy, asked me, "How much do you want to charge?" My response was, "I don't know. How much do *you* think I should charge?" He responded, "How much do you charge now?" I said, "$59 per hour." He said, "Well, you can probably charge $80 per hour and $100 on the weekend." I said, "OK, great, send me the book," and off I went into the service industry using flat-rate pricing.

> *"It's not enough to just use flat-rate pricing. To make a profit, you have to be using it at the right price and right efficiency."*

A year went by and my newfound service department lost a lot of money. I called the flat-rate company back and got the same man. I said, "What the heck? I was already losing money in new construction. I didn't need a new way to lose money." Andy's response was, "How much are you charging?" I said "$80 per hour and $100 on the weekend." He said, "You can probably charge $100 per hour and $125 on the weekend." I said, "OK, great, send me the book."

Another year went by, and my service department lost money again—not as much as the first year, but either way I was losing money and didn't have the money to lose.

So again I called Andy at the flat-rate company and asked, "OK, what should I *really* be charging?" And Andy said—you guessed it—"How much are you charging now?" I said "$100 per hour and $125 on the weekend." He said, "You could probably charge $125 per hour and $150 on the weekend."

We repeated this exercise every year until 2004, when I ran across this organization called Nexstar.

One of the first things I did with Nexstar was complete a program called "The Profit Pricer" where I discovered my breakeven was $285 per hour. I needed to be charging $325 per hour!

I called Andy at the flat-rate company back, and this time I said, "Man, why didn't you tell me I was charging way too low?" His response was now, "Where are you located?" I said, "Memphis."

Andy then said, "Oh yeah, you should be at about $350 per hour." I said, "Wow! That would have been nice to know $942,000 ago." (That was the amount my company was now in debt to my largest vendor.)

I immediately ordered new books, started training my employees to deliver a premier level of service, and started charging the right price. Five years later, I was debt-free and didn't owe anybody a dime. It's not enough to just use flat-rate pricing. To make a profit, you have to be using it at the right price and right efficiency.

3

THREE NEW RULES

There are three new rules we recommend you adopt that will immediately change your business for the better. Ready?

Rule 1: Know the person who writes the check.

Rule 2: Cash is king—get paid today.

Rule 3: How customers feel is what matters most.

Let's look at each in more detail.

■ Rule 1:
Know the Person Who Writes the Check

I know many people reading this will say, "My customers will never allow me to charge the right prices." And if your customers are home builders, general contractors, home warranty companies, home centers, and off-site property managers, you just might be right.

In all likelihood, you'll never be able to get to the right price unless you're selling to the person who actually writes the check and who will personally benefit from your good work.

To be clear, a general contractor or other business reseller will personally benefit from your work too—by paying you as little as possible to do it and pocketing the profit! The reality is these third-party agents can pay you what-ever they want or whatever they think is the going rate because you are not able to communicate the value of your services directly to their customer, the end user who is paying for everything.

You might need $2,400 for that job, but unless you are dealing with the person who writes the check, the middleman can ignore your proposal and say, "I'll pay you $1,600. Take it or leave it."

THE SUBCONTRACTOR WORK TRAP

How does this happen? Well, one of the quickest ways to get business is to do subcontracting work. It is seductive. You don't have to sell the work. The work is consistent and sometimes comes in big jobs. All you have to do is what you love, which is the work.

The problem is you'll never get ahead working for these people. To them, you're a commodity. They want the job done cheaply and efficiently. And they don't have to live with the consequences of your work for long.

So why would anyone work in a subcontractor relationship where their work is not fully valued? Here are three possible reasons:

1 • Low self-esteem, which results in the price being determined based on what someone else says your work is worth.

2 • Not learning how to get and sell customers who have a direct relationship with your company.

3 • Not knowing your financial reality and winging it. Your selling price has no basis in reality.

WORK FOR THOSE WHO WILL DIRECTLY BENEFIT

It's important to deal with the person who writes the check, because to get your $375/hour price, someone has to care about and live with the value they will receive *and* be willing to write a check for it. When you can meet one on one with the person who receives the benefit of your services, you can charge the right price.

We know how easy it is to work for a property manager or do installation work for a home center. The problem is that none of them care about the experience you provide to the end user or the quality of the work you do. Sure, they care, but not in the same way a homeowner does.

Let's say there's an office building that has a blocked drain line in the employee bathroom. If the tenants had their druthers, it would be taken care of *now*, but let's say the building manager is out of state. He is removed from the problem, so he'll want it done as cheaply as possible even if the tenants have to wait three days for it to be cleared. He is going to find a low-cost plumber and wait for him to be available.

Remember, the further you get away from the person who writes the check, the less likely it is that something good will happen. Don't be a subcontractor. Don't be even one degree separated from the person who writes the check and experiences your good work! Because if you do get that contract for 20 houses, it's going to be because you were the cheapest, and you'll be wondering why you can't get a price increase or in some cases even paid!

YOU CAN'T BEAT THE RACKET

In the early years here at Nexstar, many of the contractors who joined came from new construction work. We called them "refugees." They were sick of being beaten down on price year after year and were fleeing that life. They kept thinking they could figure out a way to beat the racket! Finally, they decided enough was enough. These new construction refugees realized that to have the life they wanted they needed to develop a customer base that truly valued their services and was willing to pay the right price.

Frank Blau Jr. also realized he could never get the price he needed doing new construction so he needed to change the business into one that would allow him to do that. He had an $8 million dollar construction company in 1971 when he completely shifted the focus of his business to residential service. No slow phaseout. He made the decision, jumped in, and changed his business to fit his life. It can be done. And if you ever want to thrive, you have to work for the right customers—the ones that write the check. Always abide by Rule 1: Know the person who writes the check.

▣ Rule 2:
Cash Is King—Get Paid Today

So often small operators are reluctant to ask for money once they've completed the job. They say, "I'll send you a bill" or "We'll worry about that later," and think that delaying payment will be interpreted as giving great service. Please stop doing this!

HOW WILL YOU BE PAYING TODAY?

Instead, try asking, "How will you be paying today?" People will understand. (And their response to this question can also help you quickly understand something about the person you're going to work for!)

When it comes to new construction, it's likely you'll get worked over on price, and even more likely you'll have to wait 90 to 120 days to get paid. Working for a low price and waiting 120 days to get paid is a terrible business model!

It doesn't have to be this way. Adopt the policy that payment for services must be received before you leave the premises—today. It is a decision you can make to not work any other way.

The reason you are hesitant to do this may be that you are embarrassed at having to charge anything at all and fear being accused of being too expensive. You think, "I'll send the invoice from home, that way I don't have to see the look on their face when they receive it."

DO, THEN GET PAID . . . TODAY

Don't wait to collect your money. Once the work is done, if the customer's choice is between keeping the money or paying you, paying you will be way down the list. The sense of urgency around the need for your services is gone, and now you will have to chase that money.

Here's another common scenario. Let's say you get a great big customer. You work for months, and then you get stuck. Either the customer goes out of business or negotiates a discount. Many unscrupulous business operators

Making the Decision to Change
Chris Corley

I started my own business essentially because I needed a job. I was the plumber in the truck who loved to fix things and make customers happy. I made all the classic money mistakes, including low price, low-margin new-construction work, and trusting my customers to pay me on time. I hired fast and fired slow and paid the price multiple times. But still I was able to make just enough money to keep the doors open and food on the table.

The problem was as I looked forward, all I could see was more of the same—general contractors looking for a lower price, low-quality employees, and the possibility that one mistake could ruin me financially. I wanted it to be different, but didn't know how to get there.

In the fall of 1996 I visited ABC Plumbing and Heating in Chicago. The purpose of the visit was to see what a successful service-only company looked like. I was blown away by its clean and organized office, trucks, and sharply dressed technicians. The owners of ABC spent time helping me discover how to price correctly, take care of a customer, and actually get paid when I was finished with the job. It was amazing! All of this was done to introduce me to a new organization named Contractors 2000 (now Nexstar).

At the end of that day I was sitting with founding member Ellen Rohr and she asked me one question that changed my life. She said, "If you don't join with us, how will your life be any different 10 or 20 years from now?"

I did join with them that very day, and my personal and business life has been remarkably different ever since.

I've still managed to make most of the mistakes mentioned in this book. But thank goodness I had peers, mentors, coaches, and training for myself and my staff to help us stay on track. Of course, none of those things would matter now if I hadn't made the decision to change. And that's what this book is all about.

are masters at taking advantage of start-up mechanical companies! Don't let it happen to you.

Terms need to be COD (cash on delivery). Get paid upon completion. Absolutely, positively do not work for people who won't agree, because you're going to get stuck, guaranteed.

Make it a priority to follow Rule 2: Cash is king—get paid today. You'll be glad you did.

■ Rule 3:
How Customers Feel Is What Matters Most

How customers feel when you are finished with the job is what matters most in the end. That's because when people buy services they don't buy often, if they feel good after the job is completed, they will feel that they received a good value.

That is also why it is so important to do work for the person writing the check. They get to experience your professionalism. You have a chance to develop rapport with them so they come to trust and like you as a human being.

All those who don't directly experience your work are interested in is the final number on your invoice.

SHOW UP ON TIME, DRESS NEATLY, SHOW RESPECT

If you show up on time, dress neatly, respect your customer and their house, and do a good job, they will feel like they got their money's worth.

But if you (and your tech) are late, act caustic or dismissive, have a bunch of racy tattoos showing, smoke inside the house, or project an air of casual indifference to their job, how do you think that will make your customer feel about you and your service?

Answer: bad.

You may think it's mainly about the work—the pipe, the panel, or the furnace—but actually, it's how you deliver the work that matters the most.

It's less about installing a light, and more about doing it in a way that makes sense and makes customers feel honored and important.

DON'T SAY ANYTHING BAD ABOUT BILL

An early Nexstar member told me a story that perfectly illustrates this point. As the owner, he was checking on a job manned by a new plumber. He walked into the basement of the customer's home and was immediately horrified. The job, which was to install some supply piping, looked, in his words, "as if a little kid had done the work!" He had never seen work so poorly performed. As a trade craftsman, he was embarrassed.

He quickly turned around to talk to the customer about redoing the work and said, "So sorry about Bill, he is new here . . ." But before he could say another word, the customer, an older woman, cut him off mid-sentence and said, "Don't you say anything bad about Bill. He was so nice to me! He is the best plumber I have ever had in my house!" The lady didn't know what a good plumbing job was supposed to look like. What was important to her was that Bill was nice to her and she felt important and understood.

Why would a customer defend that tradesman? Because it's not just about his work!

Your customers are not just buying what you are selling—they are also buying *the way you do it*. That's because there is a *psychological* component to how customers buy.

Let's face it: if someone really wants to install that water heater, there are plenty of YouTube videos out there that will walk them through it. And that's fine. Those people are probably not your customers anyway.

Your customers are people who don't want to do the job themselves. They want someone who will take care of it for them and who will make them feel good about that decision.

That's why the ultimate value of what you do is in the way you do it and how the customer feels about it at every juncture of the experience.

If you or your technicians don't get this, you can end up making your customers feel stupid. You can end up acting like you're doing the customer a favor, barking at them to get out of your way and stop questioning what you're doing.

The problem with this approach is that instead of creating a customer for life, you've just reinforced the old plumber stereotype we continue to fight to this day. (You know the one.)

It's essential that you find a way to make the customer feel listened to, important, and special. If you don't get really good at this important skill, you will not be able to charge $375/hour on a flat-rate system, which will translate into the $150,000 annual salary that will enable you to live the way you really want to live.

EXCELLENT TECHNICAL WORK IS A MINIMUM STANDARD

That said, let's be clear: the technical work you do is still the most important thing. The work has to be done right. But that is the minimum standard. When a customer calls with a service need, they expect the repair or installation to be done correctly. But ultimately, what you do that is unexpected and appreciated is what will be remembered and what will be considered when the customer reflects on their experience with you.

Do good work, but also make sure your customers feel good about the whole experience they've had with you when you leave.

Live by Rule 3: How customers feel is what matters most. ■

TIME TO GROW

■ Get out of the Truck (Work on Your Business, Not in It)

If you want to create a business that will enable you to live how you want to live, you'll also need to get out of the truck as soon as possible. You have to be in a position to work *on* your business constantly, and to be able to do that effectively, you cannot be working *in* it, too.

If you don't do this, the business will always be about you and you won't be able to grow.

Most of you love to do the work. You love working with your hands and love the freedom of being in the truck. We know that, and so we know what we're asking you to do.

We also know that, for most of you, you don't think you're very good at business. All your self-worth is wrapped up in being the world's greatest plumber, heating-cooling tech, or electrician.

It's true that running the business does not provide the same immediate feedback as working in it. That's why it's so easy to retreat back to what you love—the tools—because it provides you with an immediate sense of self-worth.

We know of some big-time PHCE businesses whose owners started out as mechanics, and whenever they get a chance to work with their hands again, their eyes light up! Over time, however, they learn to love running a business too. But we see the love of the craft in their eyes and understand the feeling they get from doing the job that they don't get as a manager or supervisor.

I know this is hard, but it must be done. If you want your business to grow, you need to get out of the truck as soon as possible.

Initially you might feel a little lost—"What did I do today?"—even though you attended to what was important to your business.

To be successful as an owner, as strange as it sounds, you have to go *away* from the thing you love. You need to put down the tools and get out of the truck or you'll hold back your business and, with it, the ability to live the way you really want to live. The only way to get out of the truck, of course, is to hire someone else to get in it.

■ Your First Hire (They've Got to Be Great)

Your first employee is the single most important person you will ever hire. That person has got to be great. We repeat: *your first hire has got to be great.* Remember that.

Sadly, the first hire for most small businesses is not so great. It's someone an owner already knows, someone who needs a job, maybe someone from church, a brother-in-law, or a friend of a friend. Even more often, an inexperienced wife or husband is drawn into the business to help relieve the pressure on the overextended spouse.

Here's the problem with this: if you get the first hire wrong, a full 50 percent of your work force will stink, and the consequences of that ratio are nearly impossible to overcome. Think about that. What if you had 100 employees and 50 of them were incompetent? The business would be destined for failure. It is the same with your first hire.

Let me magnify this even more. In a small business, employees don't have the luxury of doing just one thing. You have to do lots of things and you have to do them pretty good, too. Your first hire is not going to do just one thing. They are by necessity going to have to do multiple things. If it is your first office hire, they are going to have to be a good customer service representative, dispatcher, bookkeeper, and purchaser, among other things. If it is your first field hire, they have to be good at service, installations, sales, warranty work, and customer service.

They just have to be good. I mean *really* good.

So where do you start? What should the first hire do?

As the owner, you want to play to your strengths. Your first hire should take over responsibilities that you yourself labor to do personally. Maybe that is marketing and sales responsibilities, maybe it is the details of the office. Whatever you struggle to do at a high level—hire for those activities first.

At Nexstar, our first hire was Marla Coffin. I knew Marla—she was a good friend of my wife. I knew she was smart. I knew she had a good work ethic. I knew she was awesome at details. So I called her out of the blue and was able to recruit her to Nexstar as our second employee. She was a godsend and so talented that once we added her we weren't just doing two times the work, we were doing three times the work!

Marla was a true detail person, very thorough and consistent. She handled the billing and other important office work. She took over communications and meeting planning. She had awesome customer service skills. And she was consistent and dependable. In short, she freed me up to do what I did best, which was develop new member services and grow Nexstar faster.

The reality is that Nexstar would have struggled mightily if my first hire had been a bad one. We would have struggled even if she was average. In many respects, we got lucky finding Marla, but what I learned from the experience is never settle for average when it comes to employees. Marla was extraordinary, and, as a result, Nexstar was even better after she arrived. What I delegated to her was done even better than if I had done it myself. You should expect the same from your first hire.

If you're lucky enough, you may have married the right person or have the right brother, like Frank Blau Jr. did in Eddie. But for most people this is not the case. Most people have to work hard to find that first great employee.

So, when it comes to your first hire, don't take the path of least resistance and hire the person who needs a job or is closest to you—unless you're darn sure that person will be extraordinary. If your wife or husband is available to help but for whatever reason is not able or willing to fully commit to the business venture, leave them out of the business. Same goes for your child, sibling, or other relative.

Many small businesses fail because they hire incompetent family members for reasons that have nothing to do with what the business needs and then enable poor performance because these people are family. This not only destroys the business, but often destroys the relationship along with it.

Unfortunately, we speak from experience here. We have seen this scenario play out way too many times among the membership at Nexstar—dysfunctional family members working together in a dysfunctional business in hopelessly tangled-up relationships creating a miserable life for all involved. It is really hard to watch and one of the saddest things to see. A son bitter at a father. A wife angry at a husband. Brothers who no longer speak to each other. I am not the most sympathetic person, but seeing these things hurts me to my core.

Your business is about creating a thriving life where you can spend time and give things to the people you love. The need for careful consideration about whom you hire and why you are hiring them cannot be overstated. You need to get this right.

If you want to grow your business successfully, your first hire must be great or it won't make your life easier; it will make it much, much harder. Get this right! One more time because it's that important: *get your first hire right*.

▪ You Have to Sell It before You Can Do It

If you're like most contractors, you entered the trades because you like to work with your hands. You may even love the art and craft of what you do. You probably started out working for someone else and at some point decided you could make more money on your own. You respect the trade, but were shocked to discover that to keep the money coming in you have to sell a job before you can do it!

And, if you're like most small-business owners, you also have some baggage around the word "sales."

For many of you, the mere thought of sales triggers an image of a plaid-jacketed fast talker on the hunt for the next sucker to rip off. Or maybe you've had a few unpleasant high-pressure sales experiences that felt terrible and didn't deliver what was promised. Those people do exist. No question. And if you've experienced them, it's not tough to understand why you might perceive sales as unethical, deceptive, and even slimy. Who wants to be associated with *that*?

The good news is there is such a thing as ethical sales. In fact, sales done ethically and skillfully are essential because they're the only way a customer can learn what it is they really need to buy from you. And it's also your best opportunity to demonstrate the value of your services in a way that will allow you to charge your $375/hour rate.

The bottom line is this: to grow a strong business, you've got to master sales because you've got to sell the job before you can do it!

If you don't master sales at your company, then you'll be dependent on others outside your company to sell work on your behalf. (Cue the ominous music . . . then watch in horror as home warranty companies, general contractors, and home centers suck up your profit. Scary! Run away!!!)

Remember that nothing good happens when you depend on other people to sell your work. You will never get the right price if you are asking others to sell on your behalf. Not a chance.

Sales, the way you will do it, is simply helping customers see the alignment between their needs and the value of the services you will provide and, through that process, creating enough trust that they will want to say yes. It's a conversation, not a trick!

If you're going to have a successful contracting business, you have to make peace with the fact that *someone* in your company will need to sell your services. You either have to adapt yourself and get good at it or find an employee to sell on your behalf. Otherwise your company will underperform and you will end up doing subcontracting work for the going rate, and that's no good for anyone.

It is a big change, and if you've already got employees, one you'll have to help them manage.

You may find your great technicians are not so thrilled or willing to learn how to become great salespeople too. Some common excuses:

- They think they are above selling.
- They are introverted.
- They get satisfaction from things they create rather than from people they influence.
- Selling seems like "cheating" to them.

This is such a big deal to us that the very first member service Nexstar developed was a technician-selling program—the first of its kind.

Prior to this, all technician training in the industry was technical only. We knew this was a paradigm we had to change. We had to help our members and their employees accept the responsibility for getting customers to say "yes" for reasons other than the lowest price. (We will be forever grateful to retail sales guru Harry Friedman for helping develop Nexstar's inaugural sales and customer service training program.)

Our members soon discovered that customers would be willing to pay more for a service that was presented well, and that approach caused a seismic shift in performance across the membership.

Today, Nexstar's Service System Training is a flagship offering with more than 2,000 technicians attending annually. I look back at our first efforts and chuckle—it was groundbreaking at the time, but we have certainly come a long way in 25 years!

While our membership understands and embraces the importance of customer service and sales training to their business success, the industry is not yet quite as self-aware.

Your ability to understand and respect the need for sales is central to your ability to sell at the right price. Remember, someone has to buy before you can do the work. For that reason, learning how to get people to buy is almost more important than the work itself.

Selling is a business fundamental. It has to be mastered if your business is to succeed and thereby enable you to create the life you want. We urge you to embrace this reality and do what is needed to figure out how to make sales happen in your company as soon as possible.

■ Create Enduring Relationships

Once you've sold a job, and done work customers feel good about, the next challenge is to figure out how to maintain an ongoing relationship with them. Somehow you need to extend your ability to keep in touch beyond the initial transaction, and ensure your name stays at the top of their mind.

The goal for every job should be to consciously create a service experience that results in an expectation of routine. One way to do this is to offer customers a maintenance contract. This is your chance to make customers feel wonderful, safe, and secure knowing you'll be back in six months to make sure all is well with their systems.

At Nexstar, we did this from the jump because we knew we wanted to create something ongoing. We are an at-will organization, meaning that at any time and for any reason a member can quit Nexstar. Yet many members have been with us for more than 20 years. We are embedded into the lives of 560 contractors because of the relationships we've fostered. We know everyone's name. We remember their birthdays and their membership anniversaries. We have 45 people dedicated to cultivating members' ownership and connection with the Nexstar organization. We truly care, and it shows.

We can do this because we charge enough, but we are also obligated to do it because of the prices we charge. Think about that for a minute.

Nexstar exists solely to serve our membership. We are pure in mission and focus, and that's why we're so good. Nexstar is owned by 560 contractors—not just by our leadership—and to us, the relationship with our members is more important than the money we receive from them. This mind-set, however, creates results for Nexstar that allow us to consistently deliver extraordinary value to our members. And our members are willing to pay a fair price for our services in return.

In short, we all win. And you do, too.

Let me ask you this: What *would* you have to do to charge the right price, one that also allows you to make people feel special? And what would it take to start thinking about developing long-term relationships with your customers instead of simply doing a one-time job for them?

A good first step is this: before you show up at the next customer's home, think about what you can do to make sure their experience with you and your company is the best it can be. Then, make sure you are charging enough so that you have the time and resources required to create a long-term relationship, one that will be a source of work for many years to come *and* get you closer to living the way you really want to live. ■

5

FALLING IN LOVE WITH THE NUMBERS

The health and welfare of your business and livelihood is reflected by two documents: your income statement (also known as a profit and loss statement, or P/L) and your balance sheet.

You can't run your company for long without understanding these two documents and falling in love with the numbers on each of them. But how are you supposed to fall in love with the numbers when you've avoided math your whole life?

Granted, it's something new to learn, but I'm going to show you why it's not as hard as you might think.

■ Business Math Is Not Algebra

First, I want to make sure you're not confusing business math with algebra or other higher math functions. You'll be relieved to know that business math requires at most the ability to understand how to add, subtract, multiply, divide, and calculate percentages. Most of us learned those math skills before leaving elementary school. It's when we got to algebra that math turned into an unpleasant experience for many of us, me included.

In fact, I flunked ninth-grade algebra. I am not proud to say it, but I was lost in class. I got an F, the first ever in my life. I then went on to struggle with math through high school. I finally passed 10th-grade geometry when I was in the 12th grade. By the time I left high school I was convinced I was a math idiot and beyond hope.

As a result of these early mathematical failures, I began to avoid math and somehow managed to get through four years of college without taking any math classes whatsoever. So, if anyone understands what it's like to be intimidated by numbers, I do.

Yet in 2012, when giving a seminar at the Pumper & Cleaner Show, in front of hundreds of contractors, I was introduced as a "numbers guy." (A numbers guy who flunked ninth-grade algebra would have been a more accurate description, but I resisted the urge to correct the emcee.) I will never forget the irony of that moment.

So how did this happen? To be successful in business I knew I *had* to learn the numbers. I could not run from them anymore. I had to confront them and my own feelings of inadequacy. Frank Blau Jr. had preached the need for financial acumen in business, and so I knew I had to "take the medicine." What I discovered was that numbers as they relate to business are actually pretty easy.

I realize now that I'd allowed my "head trash" around numbers to prevent me from diving in and finding out for myself exactly what was involved!

I have long since fallen in love with the numbers in business, and if I can do it at a level high enough to be described as a "numbers guy," you can do it too.

And here's why you must. When you finally are able to understand what's happening with your company financially and you start to see the impact of your decisions play out on the balance sheet and P/L, it will cause you to make better decisions—automatically.

■ Impossible to Go Broke

Frank said, "If you fall in love with the numbers it is impossible to go broke." Here is what he means.

To get control of your business you have to know how you're doing. Are you breaking even? Are you losing money every month? How much? Watching the numbers enables you to see the rocks in the road ahead so you can steer your business around them. When you're not watching, what may have been an avoidable rock three months earlier can turn into a boulder. (Think: *We're fresh out of cash.*)

Once you have this knowledge and are monitoring your financial position monthly, unless you consciously make irresponsible or rash financial decisions, it really is almost impossible to go broke.

But more likely, when you have this knowledge and can see the impact of your financial decisions play out on paper, there's no way you'll willfully go down a path you know will cause you to go bankrupt. It becomes a negative pole.

People get in trouble financially when they stop looking at the numbers. But if you are diligent and review them monthly and own what they are telling you, Frank is right. It really *is* impossible to go broke.

I realize that when you first started the business, your goal was to pay the bills. So maybe you did that. You had an accountant do your taxes at the end of the year. In between you monitored your bank account. Things seemed to turn out OK.

You think, "OK, I'm good. No need for all this financial statement garbage. I am above it."

Allow me to tell you what *is* going to happen, because we've seen it again and again.

The cycle will continue for four, five, or six years and your business will continue to grow and become more complex. Now you have employees and inventory and trucks, and things are happening outside of your field of vision. Cash is getting low, but sales are growing so you are sure things will work out—somehow.

"We just need to get some billings out," you say.

Yet trouble is dead ahead and you don't even know it.

If you're not watching the numbers carefully and seeking to understand through percentages what is improving or degrading compared to prior months, your day of reckoning is coming.

We've seen it too many times. It is a virtual guarantee.

If you try to be the first owner to grow a great business without financials, you will end up in bankruptcy court with all the other owners who made the same mistake.

Regardless of what obstacles landed you here, you can learn the financial skills required to run a company successfully.

▉ You Can Do It

How do I know you can do it? For one thing, the math you need to know to be a master plumber and electrician or to perform a heat load on a home is much harder than the math you need to know to manage your financials.

If you can understand addition, subtraction, multiplication, division, and percentages, I promise you can manage and understand your financials.

I say *understand* your financials because all of today's financial programs do the actual calculations for you! You just have to interpret what they are telling you, and that is not hard. It is not some unique skill that only MBAs possess. All it takes is a little focus and some mentoring and you can get it.

The mere thought of math might make your body tense up, just like it did for me back in algebra when the formulas and equations were flying by. But when you overcome it, and start seeing how focusing on the numbers creates success, reviewing your monthly income statement might start to make you almost giddy. Success is exciting! And then there's the moment when you realize analyzing numbers has turned into something you're actually *good at*!

Here is the best part. When you are operating by the fundamentals outlined in this book and you have a highly profitable business, the numbers say, "Congratulations, your good work is evident here!"

It is the ultimate business adrenaline rush to get your monthly income statement and see that you crushed your net profit goals. It doesn't get any better than that.

In fact, you may find yourself looking at your financial statements weekly just to admire your good work!

Strive to understand what your financials are saying, and I predict you too *will* fall in love with your numbers—100 percent. ▉

The Going Rate Is a Math Error
Jim Hamilton

I remember Frank Blau Jr. standing at the overhead projector with a cigarette hanging out of his mouth, drawing a circle showing the costs in dollars of a hypothetical job and describing to us where the numbers come from.

He then gave us a different hypothetical job and asked us to create the selling price for it. He provided the material cost, and all our overhead and labor cost, and told us that it made up 75 percent of the selling price. It was $1,000 between material, overhead, and labor. He asked the room to come up with a selling price that would get us to 25 percent net profit on a cost of $1,000.

The room worked feverishly. Frank gave everybody about five minutes and then collected our papers—there were more than 50 of us.

One by one, Frank read the prices written on the papers: $1,250. $1,551. $2,050.

People had come up with all sorts of numbers, and very few were the same. As many contractors as there were in the room, there were almost as many answers. Remember this is a simple math equation and there is only one right answer.

After reading all the answers, Frank said, "How can this be? You all have the same cost and the same profit percentage goals, but you all come up with different prices!"

Of course, Frank knew exactly why and proceeded to teach us how to properly understand and calculate the actual selling price that day.

After that, we found out there were just *two* people out of the 50 in the room that got the proper selling price, and those two were owners of supply houses! *Zero* contractors got the price right.

Frank laughed and said, "No wonder supply houses are always trying to collect their money from contractors; they all have their heads up their asses."

JOURNEYMAN

DON'T WORRY ABOUT YOUR COMPETITORS

KEEP IT SIMPLE AND GROW WHAT YOU KNOW

BUSINESS IS A SERIES OF SYSTEMS AND PROCESSES

BUILD YOUR TEAM

WIN THE DAY

SOAR WITH EAGLES (DON'T SIT WITH BUZZARDS)

JOURNEYMAN

This section of the book builds on the last and assumes that you have done some work figuring out how you want to live, finally realize you are worth it, and know you can do this!

You've no doubt written down a budget and arrived at a realistic selling price, and you're collecting payment for your services right after they're performed. You are now out of the truck so you can start working on your business instead of in it, which is the only way it can grow. You have also made your first (great) hire, and have realized that selling is a necessary and fundamental activity for the health of your business. You're more aware of how you're making customers feel. You realize that the numbers aspect of the business isn't as hard as you thought, and you can fall in love with it because it's helping you create the life you really want and deserve.

With that foundation in place, this section presents the next series of steps you need to take. Not done with the previous steps yet? That's OK. Keep chugging away at them and keep reading. We want you to know how it all works.

DON'T WORRY ABOUT YOUR COMPETITORS

There is only one you and as such you are the only person who is qualified to decide what is best for your business. Period.

You may see one competitor add this service line and another do this kind of advertising, and you may feel as if you have to do what they are doing or you'll miss out on some opportunities. Every owner of a growing business is at some point faced with these temptations and distractions.

The way to battle this temptation is to stop and think, "What do my customers need? What do my employees need? And what are the people that I know and trust doing that I can emulate?"

In other words, "To thine own self be true."

This means you don't want to lunge at anything. Not your competitors' TV advertising (you don't know if it's working). Not their pay plan (you don't know what their total labor percentages are). Not their multiple service lines (you haven't seen their financials; they could be losing their shirts).

Don't change your business model because of what a competitor is doing, or what some expert on the Internet tells you to do, or to keep up with the Joneses. Instead, ground yourself in your own business with these four questions:

1 • "What do my customers need?"

2 • "What do my employees need?"

3 • "What are the people I know and trust doing that I can emulate?"

4 • "When I find a true mentor who has been where I have been and is having success, what do they recommend I do?"

These questions will lead you to the answers you need to decide what changes are best for your company.

Without discernment, good mentoring, and believing in yourself, you can "me-too" yourself right out of business if you're not careful.

Let's say your competitor buys all new trucks and you feel the need to keep up. You use all your cash to buy trucks, but then can't make payroll or pay your taxes so you go bankrupt. Sound silly? I have seen this specific scenario play out more than once.

There is only one you—know yourself. Stay focused on asking the right questions. And don't worry about what your competitors are doing. You'll be just fine without them. ■

The First Step Is to Believe

William B. Raymond

Lack of belief—in the selling price, in the process, and, most significantly, in oneself—is one of the biggest challenges we face as contractors. It's cloaked in statements such as: "It won't work in my market." "I'll lose all my customers." "It's not quite right." "I need to look at this just one more time."

When I first joined Nexstar, I didn't truly believe their system would work in my market. I was afraid we'd lose all of our customers. I spent three times as long as I should have perfecting everything before I implemented it (and I learned it still was flawed). I simply did not truly believe I was worth it, that the members of our team were worth it. I said I did, I thought I did, but I didn't.

Here's what I found out. What Nexstar teaches works—in small towns where everyone knows each other, in suburbs, in cities, and everywhere in between. And, at the correct selling price, the fact is you could lose half your customers and still be better off.

> *"It wasn't until I truly believed I was worth it that things began to change for the better."*

You would make more money and have happier customers and happier employees. You just need to believe and then do it.

Get to know your costs, set your correct selling price, make the phone ring, deliver great value to your customers, take care of your people, track the correct KPIs (key performance indicators), and adjust accordingly.

It's not easy. I really wrestled with this problem early in my career (and still do at times). It wasn't until I truly believed I was worth it that things began to change for the better.

After nearly 28 years of experience living this, witnessing this, and teaching this, I know it works—if you believe that you and everyone on your team are worth it. Believe now!

7

KEEP IT SIMPLE AND GROW WHAT YOU KNOW

Let's say you have a revenue goal this year of a million dollars. You might think, "I'm starting to get the hang of the plumbing service and I see how big some of these HVAC companies are. Why don't we expand our services and add HVAC?" It sounds good, but here's why you may want to rethink that strategy.

Adding a new service line can increase revenue opportunities; the problem is that it also adds an additional and *significant* layer of complexity to your business. In many cases, we've seen the premature addition of a new service line badly hurt a previously healthy contracting business. If you're considering this step, I urge you to proceed with *extreme* caution because here is what often happens when a service line is added before a business is ready.

As the owner, you shift your attention off the primary service line and onto the new service line to get it up and running. Meanwhile, the primary service line starts to go backward. Revenue growth slows and gross margins start to decline. So, while you might gain some revenue from your new HVAC line, the profit dollars you used to earn from plumbing may actually *decrease*.

For business owners with emerging companies there also is something called bandwidth that you need to keep in mind. While small and growing, a company only has the capacity or "bandwidth" to do a certain number of different things at a high level at the same time. Every company has varying degrees of bandwidth, and if you add a new service line without having enough, your business will start to leak oil. You'll find too much is going on and not all of it is getting done right. Not only does the new service line struggle, but the primary service line also starts to underperform.

That's because all trade service lines are different and thus require different strategies and tactics. A successful plumbing service company operates very differently from a successful HVAC service/replacement company, for example.

If you're looking to boost revenue, instead of adding services, find out what you're good at and figure out how to multiply and do more of *that*—first. Until you've tapped out the market, adding something new and different isn't necessarily the best growth strategy. And the reality is most owners never come close to tapping out their core market before adding these distractions.

We have Nexstar members in a *single market* from a *single location* doing well north of $30 million in HVAC, $20 million in plumbing, and $8 million in electrical services. So if you are a $1 million company in any given trade, you likely aren't even close to conquering the market share that would be required to justify adding another trade.

Adding a trade sounds like such a good idea. Your competitors are doing multiple trades—just think of the bank they must be making! And how about what that sales guy said about that hot new franchising opportunity? Bathtub refinishing—sounds exciting!

Before you go forward with any of these options, however, you need to carefully consider how your world will change if you add these things. Adding a new trade will completely and radically change the world as you know it. (And not necessarily in a good way.)

For example, let's say you are used to selling and doing demand service (break/fix). You go in, see what's wrong, give the customer some options, and do the repair. The customer is happy. The customer pays you. That's what you're good at.

Your people are also good at selling that break/fix service and diagnosing those problems.

You might think that adding something like bathtub refinishing is a no-brainer. Why not? Your plumber is there to do diagnosis and repair, so why can't he talk to the customer about refinishing the tub too?

The problem with this approach is that tub refinishing is a different type of sale with different customer motivation. The motivation for refinishing a tub comes from a different place than the motivation to fix a broken toilet or a leaky faucet.

Asking your plumbers to navigate these different customer motivations creates another layer of complexity for them, one your business as currently structured might not be able to handle.

All we're saying here is make it a point to prove to yourself that you've maxed out your core business and all market share opportunities before you add something noncore to the mix. Or all you may end up doing is harming your core business and needlessly complicating your life.

Nexstar is no different. We know we are good at serving companies who perform service and replacement work. But just like some of you, we have thought about extending our services to other types of contractors in other industries. The allure of that idea is intense! My ego says we can do it. Some days I even feel a little bored with the mechanical trades and hanker for something new to sink my teeth into.

But here is what we know: Nexstar is not even close to helping all PHCE businesses reach their potential. We know what we are good at; we repeat it consistently based on a very tight business strategy and execute processes that have delivered success for us time and again. Our current industries are huge! And just like you, Nexstar also has a certain bandwidth. So until we are comfortable knowing that we have maxed out our work in the PHCE industries and we are strong enough as an organization to jump into a new industry without detracting from our core business, we are going to stay right here and continue doing what we do best.

Save yourself from needless stress, heartache, and diminished business performance. Before you add any new service line, make doubly sure you have maxed out the potential of your core business first. ▩

Homeowners See the Value

Jim Hamilton

When I attended Frank Blau Jr.'s "The Business of Contracting" seminar, he taught us how to come up with the proper selling price. At one point I turned to him and asked, "How can I do this in new construction?" I was a new-construction plumber at the time. Frank walked toward me as I was asking the question, but he turned away as he heard the message. Then he spun back around, gave me the sign of the cross, and said, "You can't!"

He continued, "You can't sell value to a bean counter. If a customer values the dollar more than the service you are providing, you're going to lose out to the lowest-priced guy. You saw the example in this class of contractors coming up with multiple selling prices for one problem, and that one math problem has only one correct selling price. So you're competing with contractors that have their heads up their asses!"

Frank started chuckling, and I got nervous because I realized he was right!

The only way to get the price you need is to sell to the customer that owns the work you're going to perform. The owner is the one who will see the value in the work you're about to do.

"The only way to get the price you need is to sell to the customer that owns the work you're going to perform."

In that moment, I knew I had to get out of new construction. Three days later, I found myself in Milwaukee, in Frank's office, looking at the Blau business model, riding in the trucks with his "technicians" (not plumbers), and spending more time watching his business humming along making nothing but money!

8

BUSINESS IS A SERIES OF SYSTEMS AND PROCESSES

A well-run business leans on a combination of systems that fit neatly within each other. And each system is composed of a series of processes that are repeated and repeatable.

The good news is many of these systems and processes already exist. The bad news is they are all locked up inside your head! You instinctively know what to do, and you do it.

The problem with this approach is your employees can't read your mind, and so without knowing your system they end up doing things their own way, which likely won't be your way.

If you want other people to help you grow the business your way, your systems need to be documented, and you have to train people on them. It's the *only* way you'll be able to successfully grow the business beyond yourself.

You want to go from "I know how to do this" to enabling others to know how to do it, too. And the most efficient way to do that is to document what you know and share it.

Sure, you can train people without documenting your systems and processes. The only problem with this method is it takes a long, long time and you need to always be present.

To teach someone how to plumb, for example, they can ride with you and observe what you're doing, and they'll be a competent plumber in about three years. That's OK if your goal is to hire one plumber—maybe it's your son—but if you want to grow a business, you are going to have to speed that process up. Documented processes are the way to do that.

Your job is to document how everything gets done in your business, from opening the shop in the morning to turning the phones over to the on-call person at night, and everything in between.

If you want to grow a business, you have to document your processes. There is no way around it. It is tedious work, but until you do it, your business won't be able to grow.

If you're freaking out at the thought of this, don't. You can hire someone to help you do it. Let them interview you and commit what you say to paper. (Just don't forget to check their work!)

The point is, not being good at writing or documenting information doesn't get you off the hook. To grow a business that will enable you to live the way you want to live, you have to figure out a way to get it done.

Nexstar accelerates this kind of work for its members because we've already created documentation for all the core business systems required for a service and replacement contracting business. But even if you have to start from scratch, get going. You will not be able to grow a business beyond yourself until you get this important work done.

In a great company, the owner, from the comfort of his or her office, can tell you what's happening in the dispatch office at 7:30 a.m. on Tuesday, along with who is there, what they're talking about, and the intentionality of their actions.

The owner can do this because everyone has been trained in a dynamic daily routine based on documented systems and processes. Employees know what is expected of them. And they want to do it because performing the routine provides them with a sense of purpose and security that the business is headed in the right direction and will continue to benefit them and everyone working in it.

Translating systems and processes into a dynamic daily routine helps you maintain the company's momentum and provides the energy and enthusiasm needed to sustain everyone working in it. ■

9

BUILD YOUR TEAM

One key to success is to pay top people well to do extraordinary work. Be a leader in pay. Make the pay so good that people would really have to take a financial hit to go into business themselves instead of achieving their financial goals with you.

■ Pay Them Well and They Will Come . . . and Stay

Show people what you contribute into profit sharing, and what that will mean to them at 65 years old. Provide great benefits so they don't have to leave you to get top-notch health care or secure their retirement.

You want your top producers thinking, "Do I really want to leave all of this to go into business myself?"

If you've got a top technician making $120,000 a year with great benefits, they likely will not want to leave and go into business. But if that same top technician is only making $55,000 a year with no clear idea of how to make more money with you, it's not as hard to walk out and hang out a shingle.

At first, most people react to this advice with, "Where is the money going to come from to pay out all this to employees?" The answer is if you legitimately need something in your business, you have to build it into your selling price.

And you are going to need a stable, experienced, well-trained workforce if you're going to build the kind of company that will grow and enable you to live how you want to live. Don't cut corners here. Be the leader in pay and benefits and know that your customers need great people and—as Frank Blau Jr. said—it is in their best interest to pay for them!

■ Manage, Don't Do

As you scale a business up and start to add people, there will be one major tendency you'll fight, which is not delegating work to others. If you are like the typical owner in this business, you are good at getting things done yourself. In fact, if you started your business from scratch, I am going to bet you're a jack-of-all-trades superstar.

Here is the reality. People you hire won't always do the delegated task quite as well as you would. This is especially true if you are a stellar technician and consider craftsmanship your greatest strength. You will hear negative feedback from customers and employees who were used to working directly with you. They will complain about not working with you anymore and, truth be told, that is good to hear. You are missed!

Again, if you've helped your business reach this point, you are a pretty good personal performer. Remember, however, that you can't measure every employee against perfection—or against yourself.

Maybe you're the world's best mechanic, and your employees are good but not as good as you. Your challenge is in accepting that your employees might do things differently than you do, because if you insist on exact duplication (aka perfection) you won't be able to grow your company.

If this is not you, this advice might sound silly, but we have seen dozens of owners believe that no one could do the job like they could and they just couldn't grow a business as a result.

Let's get used to the idea that you have to learn how to delegate responsibilities and accept that people will do things differently and maybe in some cases not as well as you. So what do you delegate and what do you keep in a growing business?

The first step is to know what you're great at and what you're really bad at and try to hire people to do the things that you are bad at or that don't come easily to you. This sounds like simple advice, but it is not always followed.

Forget about what others have delegated first; you need to understand your own strengths in order to make this decision for you and you only.

For example, I know I'm not great at organizing and maintaining a variety of details, so I make a point to hire people who are good at that and surround myself with those people. It ensures that things get done and keeps me from getting bogged down on tasks I'm not good at and don't look forward to doing. This is the first step to decentralizing authority in your business. Decentralize things you struggle with first—fieldwork, sales leadership, details, etc.

Play to your strengths while acknowledging—but not obsessing over—correcting your weaknesses. Figure out what your strengths are and focus on those; delegate your weaknesses. Here is the beauty of growing a business. When it is just you, you must do *everything* to keep the doors open, including things you don't enjoy. As you grow and start to delegate responsibilities, you get to shed the tasks that are not enjoyable. That alone is incentive to grow in my opinion. If I had to enter invoices or sort fittings every day for the rest of my life, I would purposely walk into traffic. There's no way I'd want to stay small and have to do those tasks forever!

Neglecting to delegate is the downfall of many emerging companies but there is a right way to do it. You have to have core values in your business, but your approach to work and the work of others needs to be one of appreciation and tolerance. You also want to surround yourself with people that you will enjoy seeing every day. That means you need to have some level of affinity for them. At the same time, you want to have a strong tolerance for people who are different from you. For example, if you are a very extroverted person, you might have to work on getting used to a person who is more quiet and needs their space.

In delegating, even though you no longer have to do the task, as the owner you still have to verify it has been done and that means inspecting the work of the person you delegated it to. Delegation is not the same as abdication! You might not be doing the task, but you're still responsible for the outcome. The pain of thinking something was getting done only to find out it was not is so great for owners that they may refuse to ever delegate again, guaranteeing a small, owner-dependent business. Don't let it happen to you. Inspect what you expect!

Some people will feel offended by this inspection and say, "Don't you trust me?" The natural reaction to this (and the one they are secretly hoping for) is, "Well, I do trust you, so I'm not going to check." This is a huge mistake because your job as a manager is to verify that important critical tasks have been done.

The way to overcome this awkward moment is to put systems in place and train people on them. Then take time to communicate that while you do trust your people, getting these tasks done is very important, and it's your responsibility to make sure they're done so the company can move forward and everyone can win.

The consequences of not inspecting delegated work can be serious. What if you delegate the books to someone only to discover a white-hot mess when that person goes on vacation or quits—a file folder of unpaid invoices or worse?

This and other unwelcome scenarios are 100 percent preventable if you establish a policy and put a system in place that enables you to check people's work.

When the job is not done or is done incorrectly, you need a review process that lets you know these things are occurring so you can act quickly.

You have to have systems and processes in place and lay them all out at the beginning. Explain: "This is how it works. Having the same process for everyone will enable us to catch problems early, which is better for all of us."

Go through and practice saying the words, "It's not that I don't trust you. This is important, and I need to make sure we're on the same page!"

And do it across the board. Everyone goes through each week's activity with the boss. It's just a responsible business practice. Remember: delegate, don't abdicate.

■ Make Sure Superstars Can Thrive (And the Mediocre Get Gone)

We talked about how your first hire has to be great, otherwise 50 percent of the employees in your company will stink. When that's the case, things can go south quick.

As you add five, then 10, then 25 people, your business won't fall apart if you accidentally hire one mediocre person.

The new problem will be that as your company gets bigger, that same mediocre person can kind of hide out and blend in. As your staff gets larger, there is not as much accountability per person as there is with just a two- or three-person company.

But if you don't get on top of this, what happens is the idea that being mediocre is OK becomes part of your business's DNA. You end up with a quiet underlying assumption that employees can't get fired for being just OK; the only way to be fired is to do something *really bad*.

Your superstar performers will resent this. They will also resent policies you put in place to try to prevent the mediocre people from doing their thing, which is to slack off.

For example, a mediocre employee is constantly late so you make a decree—"Everyone will be here at 8:00 a.m."—to prevent the company from getting cheated by a few scofflaws.

When you're a superstar, this is not fun. *Especially* if you're that person who routinely stays the extra 20 minutes after quitting time to get the work out.

No superstar I know likes restrictions, or being micromanaged, because one of the qualities of superstars is that they are *responsible for results*. They are almost always there by 8:00 a.m. anyway, but the fact that they are being told they *must* be there at eight is an irritant that can get under their skin. I know that does not make much sense, but ask any performer if they like being told what they can and can't do and then brace yourself for the answer.

Here is how to handle this problem. Don't settle for mediocre. Get rid of those mediocre people! Otherwise, as you scale the business, you'll have four kick-ass customer service agents answering the phone, and one who is nice but causes all kinds of drama.

You might think, "Well, the other four are good, we can cover for her." Don't do that!

Too many mediocre employees can cause the death of a business when it gets to a certain size.

The Right People
Jim Hamilton

I started my service contracting business three months after I met Frank Blau Jr. on June 2, 1990. After seeing Frank's business, I knew this was going to be a successful venture, so I purchased two trucks and hired a service plumber. I knew all the guys in town and so I knew who was good. My first plumber and I were the only employees in the business.

I had a bag phone and answered all my calls from the field. We had two-way radios in the trucks, and I would get on the radio and dispatch the other plumber as I answered the incoming phone calls myself.

This went on for two months when I realized that my phone was ringing more and more. I needed to hire a second person to be a dispatcher/customer service representative, somebody to come in, answer the phones, and dispatch myself and the other plumber to the jobs.

I knew a man, Mike, who worked hard and was in a dead-end job as a truck driver for a supply house. I figured if he was dropping off tubs at new construction houses with no addresses, he could find his way around town and make sure we were dispatched in the right direction.

Mike was an essential employee for me and my best hire. He continued with my business and eventually became my operations manager.

After another month, Frank told me to get out of the truck. So I hired another plumber. Again, I had an advantage because I knew all the good plumbers in town and I paid the most. Thanks to Frank, I emulated his business 100 percent, all the way down to the Blau logo.

It's important that you hire the best people, because if any of those employees had quit on me early on, I may still be in the truck today. Another pearl of wisdom Frank gave me: "Pay your employees so well that they can't afford to leave you." This doesn't mean they have the right to stay, however, if they underperform. In fact, one of my favorite sayings I also took from Frank: "If you don't perform well, your ass is grass and I'm the lawn mower."

■ Rules, Rules, and More Rules

When it comes to your business, there's a natural arc that occurs, which is that you go from no rules at all to having way too many rules. It's OK to have business rules so you have uniformity. There can't be anarchy.

The problem occurs when you create rules in an attempt to manage a few mediocre people that you should be managing in another way, such as one-on-one coaching, or, if that doesn't work, firing.

When instituting any new restrictive policy, ask yourself, "Why am I doing this? Is it for everyone or is it because of a few people on my team that keep cutting corners?"

If there are just a few problem people, get them in your office and address the issues directly with them. Don't hide behind an ever-expanding manual of policies because you don't have the nerve to sit people down and have a hard conversation.

If you've got someone hiding out in your business and cutting corners, ask yourself, "What do I have to do with this person so I'm not settling for average?" Worry about the bottom 10 percent of employees and quit fussing with the 90 percent.

Do businesses need everyone to be extraordinary? No. But what if they were? Think about it. How much easier would your life be, and the lives of your coworkers? How much better would other people's performance be, if they didn't have to carry any dead weight?

Decide right now, "I'm not going to settle for average employees in any role anymore." Hire great people and pay them well, and they will stay. And your customers will pay for it all because it is in their best interest to do so.

Remember, in business there will always be conflict. That is just life. You already made peace with the conflict of customers complaining that your price is too high a long time ago. Dealing with underperforming employees is another one of those conflicts. For most owners, the conflict of having employees you have to confront sometimes is better than the conflict created by having to do everything yourself and not being able to grow.

This conflict persists when you fail to make necessary decisions about the mediocre. Worse, eventually your good people notice, and they start to resent it.

When people are jerks or outright scofflaws, they are easy to fire. A guy comes to work drunk and out he goes. It's much tougher when people are pleasant but just not getting the job done at a high level.

The problem with keeping underperformers is that you are holding back your other employees by maintaining that weak link in the chain. No one wants to be held back by someone who isn't effective.

You want to grow people, but there are times when it doesn't work anymore for a number of reasons. You might feel like you have to keep someone out of loyalty. But if you want to keep your superstar employees, you can't accept underperformance—from anyone. ■

CHAPTER

10

WIN THE DAY

When I go into a business that is struggling, one of the first things I say to the company leaders is, "Define success for me in your role today."

Invariably, people say, "My job is to make sure my customers are happy and the guys in the field are supported."

When we check that out, sure enough, leaders are doing just that. All the way. Even if the business is losing money and revenue is down 50 percent, everyone is making sure customers are happy and the employees are supported. It would seem success in achieving that goal is subject to personal interpretation.

What they usually don't know (yet) is that the correct answer goes something like this: "Each of my five technicians needs to bring in $1,000 in business per day. My goal is to bring in a total of $5,000 of business per day, and to make sure we achieve that goal I will make sure my techs have what they need to be successful."

That is the right answer. The goal of the day is $5,000. That is "winning the day."

Here is what is wrong with the first answer. There is no way to know if you are successful. You can work your tail off trying to make customers happy and support the guys in the field and still go bankrupt.

The reality of a demand service business is that most companies let the day run them rather than them running the day. There is a lot of victim thinking that can go on:

"It is too mild out."

"Calls are slow because people are waiting for their tax refund."

"If only I had more calls . . ."

"It is election season. Everyone is afraid to spend money."

These common excuses for poor business performance put the responsibility for success on forces outside the business that you can't control.

That is a hideous way to live. It feels good to say it, however, because then you don't feel bad when you perform poorly. You say, "It's not my fault!" The reality is that this is more head trash.

Successful business operators don't buy these excuses. The reason you need great leaders in a business is to make adjustments so you achieve business success when the weather or politics or whatever is not on your side. If it was all about the weather, then you would not need daily management.

So, if I'm a company leader, and at 2:00 p.m. it starts looking like I won't get to $5,000, I start to "contort" the business. With a clear understanding of what success means *today*, I know it is my job to take aim at getting in at least $5,000 before the close of business. At this point, my job is not just about delighting customers or supporting the guys in the field because that's impossible to measure. It is about achieving the goal today. I create calls through outbound calling to fill the empty call board. I call technicians before sending them on remaining jobs to remind them of customer service opportunities. In short, I do what is necessary to win the day so that when I shut the door, I know that I won.

Most contractors and employees measure success by how hard they are working. The problem with working 10 or 12 or 14 hours a day is that it's too easy to run yourself ragged even as your financial goals are not being met.

It doesn't have to be this way.

Home service is a *daily receipts business*, and if you don't have that mindset you can get in real trouble! The good news is if yesterday was bad, you can put it behind you. You can change the next day. It is a whole new opportunity to win. With many industries, it takes months to change prices, processes, and results. Not in the home service business. We can change things tomorrow for the better.

The change that happens when you accept this and start playing to it can be monumental. So that's really what we mean by the statement "win the day."

Establish a quantifiable goal for the business and each production role in the company. The impact of this approach is huge and game changing. Then focus on winning each day of the week. This mind-set will change everything for the better. ∎

11

SOAR WITH EAGLES (DON'T SIT WITH BUZZARDS)

You are the average of the five people you spend the most time with, according to business and inspirational speaker Jim Rohn. And research shows you probably make within 10 percent of what most of the people you hang out with are making. Depending on who you spend time with that statement is either comforting or terrifying! (Thinking back on my college buddies, it's pretty obvious to me now why I was so drunk, ignorant, and broke back then!)

■ Surround Yourself with Those Who Are Aspiring

To influence this ratio, you really want to surround yourself with people who are inspiring and aspiring. Seek to surround yourself with people who not only want but also have the capacity to achieve big things.

Don't worry. Everyone has ne'er-do-well friends, people who are still kind of out there cutting corners in life. They can stay. They just can't be the only people you're hanging out with!

In business especially, you want to be around people you look up to and who are going after great things. It's pretty tough to be the only one shooting for extraordinary when everyone around you is settling for whatever life hands them.

In business, you have choices that you don't have when it comes to your family. For example, you can choose what industry events you attend and you can choose who your peers are. You can seek out amazing people that inspire you and who you can inspire as well. On the other hand, you don't always have as much choice when it comes to the folks who are sitting at the Thanksgiving table with you.

When you select your peers, you can watch what great things they create, which inspires you to create great things, too.

It's easy to set lofty business goals. But when you know you're going to be in regular contact with these high achievers, you'll be more motivated to take action toward those goals so you'll have great things to report too. It's a little friendly competition that helps everyone get and stay in action. (That is also the beauty of Nexstar—aspiring contractors getting together and inspiring each other to greater heights!)

To achieve great things in your business, strive to soar with eagles instead of sitting on branches with buzzards.

■ Be-Do-Have

Be-do-have is shorthand for a phrase that originated with the great motivator and teacher Zig Ziglar. The whole phrase is, "You've got to *be* before you can do and *do* before you can *have*." This approach works in all aspects of life, but at Nexstar we apply the philosophy this way:

If you want to have a successful contracting business then you first have to *be*, meaning actually adopt the *identity* of a person who has a successful business. You have to start thinking of yourself as a person who owns a successful contracting company.

Observe how a successful person thinks, how they dress, who they spend time with—and then become that person.

As you become that person, you will then begin to *do* the things that person would do to be successful. You will emulate successful people you know. You will listen to mentors who are successful and take their advice. You will discard old destructive habits and adopt new daily routines that will create success.

Then, and only then, will you be able to *have* a successful business. Remember it's be-do-have—in that order.

BE	DO	HAVE
Be a highly successful business owner who is worth it and deserves a thriving business and a good income.	*Do* all the things that a highly successful business owner does.	*Have* a successful PHCE contracting business and the ability to live the way you really want to live.

Most people have this exactly backward. They believe they will *feel* like they deserve a thriving business and finally *be* a successful business owner once they are successful.

It doesn't work that way! To create success, you have to *be* a person who believes you are worthy of success first. You have to adopt that identity because only then will you be compelled to do what is required to create a successful PHCE business and a good life for you, your family, and your employees. ■

MASTER

IN SEARCH OF A NEW "WHY"

SUCCESS TRAPS

BUILDING LEADERS

LEADERSHIP WISDOM

MASTER

At the master level, you have built a marquee PHCE brand. You have achieved your personal financial goals, and creature comforts and financial security are no longer an issue for you. Congratulations!

Take pride in this accomplishment, but beware. It is at this very point that your passion for the business may also start to wane because the original reason why you went into business is perhaps no longer valid.

A select few contractors who reach this level never lose their passion. For them business is a game, not a means to an end. Doing business is itself a motivation, and for these people being the owner of a successful, growing company is their identity. They do not have hobbies or other interests that pull them away from the business.

However, if the above does not describe you and your motivation, it is at this point that the business and everyone in it—all that you have worked so hard for—may start to suffer. To get your passion back, you'll have to do some soul searching. You'll need to find a new reason to be in business, a new "why." One that is bigger than the one you had before. One that inspires the business growth and leadership development that will enable you to do a great service to your employees and leave an amazing legacy.

When you reach the master level, you have the unique opportunity and privilege of impacting not just an industry but also a community, and—depending on the new "why" you choose—the world. Big stuff. Let's find out how.

12

IN SEARCH OF A NEW "WHY"

R eaching the point in business where your financial needs have been met and your business can essentially run without you is a big goal for most owners, and achieving that goal is deserving of celebration.

What you probably don't realize is once you reach that point you will be faced with a whole new set of challenges.

One of those challenges is how to keep it going. Especially when you don't feel like being at the office 50 hours a week anymore—and your business is constructed in a way that, technically, you don't have to be.

This is a risky time for you and your business. Riskier than you may think.

When you first got into business, your first "why" was likely that you wanted to make money! Your big dream was to make enough income to support your family.

Next, you focused on building up your business to secure your future.

All those things provided you with plenty of motivation to get up in the morning and work on the business.

At the master level, all your original motivations have been fulfilled. Without a fresh "why" to drive you forward, the risk is the business will begin to suffer because the energy you used to pump into it every day is now going elsewhere, perhaps hobbies. More often, however, it sparks a midlife crisis that leads to less positive pursuits. (Think: a gray-haired guy with a ponytail in a red convertible with a young blond next to him.)

To keep this crisis from happening, you need to make a conscious effort to renew your passion for the business. You need to reenvision the reason why you are in business because it has changed.

Let me explain.

The day I quit my job in 1992 to become Nexstar's first employee was the same day I took my wife Barbara home from the hospital with our second child, a son, Brent. At age 30, I had a two-year-old girl (Lauren) and a new son. In short, I had a lot of responsibilities.

Frank Blau Jr. offered me a $45,000 a year salary, which was a big increase over my prior job. This job allowed my wife to stay home and raise our children and live in relative comfort. So when Frank offered me the job, I jumped at it!

At that time, I was a professional nobody and I could not go find another $45,000 a year job very easily. The reality is Frank could have offered me a job in an asbestos factory and I would have taken it for that salary. Forget the mission of Nexstar. My "why" was I had a family to support!

But it was more than that. I wanted to make a professional name for myself. I wanted more than an average career. Nexstar was a very public job, and failure meant *public* failure—not just for the organization, but also for me personally.

I *had* to succeed at Nexstar. It was a career make or break for me. Failure was not an option. Professional success that would allow me to take care of my family so we could live the way we wanted to live was my "why." So was creating a name for myself as a successful executive; I wanted that as my identity. These were two very powerful motivators.

Sure, I believed in the mission of Nexstar and I did not want to let Frank down. But make no mistake: I would have worked hard to retain any job that would allow me to support my family and advance my career. My early "why" was personal, and in many ways selfish.

Fast-forward 20 or so years. My children are out of the house. I've been blessed with a great career and I have made a name for myself in this industry. My original "why" has been satisfied.

Over time, however, I noticed it was tougher to get up early and work late. It was taking more and more effort to engage and work as hard as I did when I was in my mid-30s. I was kind of struggling and I really didn't know why. All the little problems in business seemed so much more irritating. There were days when I felt like going golfing instead of confronting yet another set of challenges in the business.

Shiny Objects
Julian Scadden

It was the spring of 2009, and while other businesses were going under, the plumbing company where I served as operations manager was coming off a record growth year in our residential service business. We thought it was time to take advantage of the slumping market by acquiring a company.

As a plumbing business, we wanted to add HVAC by acquiring at least one of the local companies that we knew to be going out of business. We were in our first year of Nexstar membership and ran the idea by our business coach Jack Tester. With one look at our income statement, Jack asked a simple question: "Where are the sewer sales broken out?" We had all plumbing lumped together, so there was no way to know how profitable (or not) our sewer sales were. He encouraged us to wait on the acquisitions and work on growing the sewer business first.

The owner of the business, however, was not to be swayed from the HVAC dream. He tasked me with separating plumbing and sewer into two divisions, while he pursued adding HVAC. Within three months of job costing our sewer jobs, our company revenue jumped by 18 percent over the prior year. We learned how to maximize leads and provide multiple options on drain work from repair, jetting, lining, and replacement. Our plumbing service also became more profitable as the service manager could manage labor, materials, and other expenses for his department more clearly. Everything was coming up a winner—except for our HVAC expansion.

For almost a year, all the profit from our plumbing and sewer sales fed that HVAC department—until we found the right person to run it.

Over the next few years, HVAC did become profitable for us, but we put the business in a very lean year of stress because of our haste to add a service line. We could have waited a year and planned strategically to springboard success.

Take it from me—we were fortunate to survive! A few twists and turns differently and we very well could have gone out of business chasing what we wanted instead of perfecting what we already knew first.

Eventually, I realized what it was. My original "why" was no longer driving me. I had to find a new one!

But how?

Finding a new "why" took some introspection. It did not come to me in a lightning bolt of clarity. It took shape over time.

I came to realize that as CEO, when I do a great job and Nexstar is strong and effective, it provides an opportunity for members to change their lives and the lives of their employees. I own this responsibility; I am filled with gratitude when I see lives change for the better and know that I played some small role in it.

The better I am as the CEO of Nexstar, the more lives Nexstar changes. Do a great job—help change a lot of lives. Do an average job—change fewer lives. Heady stuff!

When an owner finally "gets it" and is enjoying the benefits and prestige of owning a growing business, or when I see the light go on in the eyes of someone in one of our training programs, I know they have been changed and they will be a better person for their affiliation with Nexstar.

Also, I want to make sure Nexstar is growing and vital so it can provide opportunities for our amazing employees in the same way Frank and Nexstar did for me.

Helping people change their lives is my new "why." Very different from when I was 30, but just as compelling—perhaps even more so!

Finding my new "why" took some time. I had to really think it through. And I had to not only believe it, but also be able to *own* it.

Now when the alarm goes off at 5:15 a.m., I know exactly why I am getting up so early. And if I struggle to throw off the covers and get going, I think back to my responsibilities and the opportunity I have to help people improve their lives.

I remember my "why."

You have to address this issue because without a compelling "why" to serve, you will drift further and further away from your business. You will lose the motivation to work hard, and your business will stall out. And when this happens, your employees and customers will suffer, along with your legacy.

If you've tapped out your original "why," you need to refresh it so it can provide you with the energy and focus needed to maintain the momentum and build on the success that you and your employees have invested so many years in creating.

To get to this point in business you had to be *extraordinary*. To keep going, you have to find a new reason to remain that way.

Finding this new "why" will require you to strip away some selfishness. To get in touch with who and what it is you think of beyond yourself and your family. To find a new answer to the most important question in business: Why should I be extraordinary today?

Transitioning your "why" from improving your life and the lives of your family to improving the lives of your employees and their families—or other greater goals—can be just as exciting and rewarding as meeting your personal hierarchy of needs.

For me, it's deeply gratifying to look into the eyes of people working for Nexstar and see them growing from workers to true professionals. It is exciting to hear about the exotic vacations they can now take or the house they just bought. It is fun to see them grasp the mission and purpose of Nexstar and feel the satisfaction of our contribution to a great cause.

I also know that based on my current "why" if I decide to give *less* than full effort because my needs are already met, I'm cheating my employees!

Are you still giving full effort? Are you still extraordinary?

If you're going to succeed at the master level, nothing short of full effort will suffice. Your employees deserve nothing less.

So, how solid *is* your "why"? Does it motivate you as much or more than your original "why"?

At this stage, you must do what it takes to find a new "why" or take steps to get out of the business. There is no middle path. ▪

SUCCESS TRAPS

At the master level, there are a few success traps that can really get you in trouble if they aren't avoided or caught early and corrected. They show up in the form of unproductive attitudes and faulty thinking. Here are three of the biggest ones:

1 • Thinking you can coast, work from the beach, and just deposit the checks.

2 • Thinking you are finished growing and learning as a person and a leader.

3 • Thinking you are done with change.

■ Trap 1:
I Can Work from the Beach and Take It Easy

You might think you can hire great leaders, hand them the documented systems, and then proceed to live an amazing life on the beach lounging in a hammock and dreaming about what to do with the reams of cash coming in from your company. Easy mailbox money.

Unfortunately, this is a myth, and a dangerous one. And anyone who tells you different has not managed people for very long or very effectively.

That's because people at all levels in your company are tuned in to what you believe, and they are very sensitive to whether your actions are aligned with those beliefs. Employees will rarely work any harder than the boss does, and if you ask them to do something more than you are willing to do, they won't do it for long.

That means an approach of "Here are the keys; I am going to enjoy the good life while you work hard" won't cut it. No one wants to work hard to enrich someone who is on permanent vacation at the beach.

You don't have to be a slave to the business. But you do have to continue to run the business in an inspired, engaged way. (Remember your "why"!)

Owning a business is not like buying an investment in the stock market. That company doesn't care what you do. Their employees don't even know your name. Yours do! Your employees are always looking to you for guidance. They are listening to what you say and, more importantly, they are watching everything you do.

If you still have the title and people are looking to you as the leader of the business, you can't give anything less than full effort. You can't take all the money and authority, go on permanent vacation, and expect the business to continue to prosper, because it won't.

Like it or not, unless you've done some serious and intentional succession planning, you are the special ingredient that makes your company unique.

Special ingredient? What?

Bear with me.

In the early days of Nexstar, we had a man named Frank MaGuire in to talk about leadership. He was an executive on the team that built the Kentucky Fried Chicken empire. He told us a story about when Colonel Harland Sanders finally sold the business to investors. The key to the sale was the closely guarded blend of 11 secret ingredients in his fried chicken recipe.

The sale was complete with the signing of the final documents, and everyone was at the conference table exchanging information—including the 11 secret ingredients. After reviewing the recipe, the new owner turned to Sanders and said in a concerned voice, "There are only 10 ingredients here. What is the 11th ingredient?"

Sanders stared the new owner right in the face, slowly pointed his finger at his own chest, and said with all the certainty in the world, "It is right here."

It was him! Sanders recognized that his passion and vision for KFC was just as big a factor in its success as the remaining 10 ingredients in his fried chicken recipe.

This was an important lesson I've never forgotten on the incredible value of inspired leadership.

Your inspired leadership is the secret ingredient to your success and it is more important now than ever.

If you do decide to back off in the business, whoever is taking your place better also have that special ingredient or all you've worked for may be lost—which brings us to another facet of this trap.

I'LL JUST HIRE SOMEONE WHO THINKS LIKE AN OWNER

Why did you put in all the hard work, engage in the tough conversations, and endure the sleepless nights that come with growing a successful business?

Because of your "why."

If your "why" drove you to be extraordinary, when you're ready to step down, you better get someone in there who aspires to be extraordinary too. Someone who has a compelling "why" that is in alignment with yours and drives them as hard as your "why" drove you.

How do you do that? First, make sure the same incentives and motivations you had are in place for the person you are asking to play your old role.

I once had the pleasure of hearing serial entrepreneur Ari Weinzweig, cofounder of the Zingerman Community of Businesses in Ann Arbor, Michigan, at a *Fortune Magazine*/Gazelle conference. In talking to us about turning the business over to someone else to run, he said, "You don't want someone running a business who thinks like an owner; you want them to *be* an owner." It's an interesting distinction.

Over the years, I have heard many failed managers utter the phrase, "But I am running this place like I owned it!" At the same time, businesses are hemorrhaging cash and it is apparent the managers are giving less than full effort.

It's not enough that someone thinks like an owner if they aren't invested in the same way you are.

Remember what motivated you. Sure, it was the potential for success, but it was also the fear of failure and financial loss.

As an owner, failure almost always results in some kind of personal hardship. When times get tough, you have to figure out a way to get through it. You can't just give two weeks' notice and walk away in the same way an employee can!

The person who will be able to take over for you will be special and rare. Until you have that person in place with the right personal incentives, *and* they have willingly accepted the right amount of personal risk, *and* you are convinced their personal "why" is in alignment with yours, you can't remove yourself from the business without creating some serious consequences.

YOUR BUSINESS IS EITHER GROWING OR DYING

Another facet of this "work at the beach" trap is thinking that because the business is successful you can ride on its coattails without investing any more of your time or effort. That you can finally coast.

The problem is that's not true.

In business, you're either growing or you're dying. If you're coasting, I've got news for you. The business is dying. And it won't take your people very long to sniff that out.

Here's the thing: your employees have to believe that tomorrow will be better than today. The moment they realize there is no more room for them to grow personally because the company isn't growing anymore is the moment they will begin to check out. First mentally, and then physically.

No one will say it out loud, but this feeling will start to show itself in less than full effort and low morale. Then, over time, your good employees will slowly leave for greener pastures.

The real reasons they are disengaged or leaving may be masked with simple rationalizations, such as, "He just didn't want to be on call anymore" or "She decided work was no longer a priority and wanted to spend more time at home with the dogs."

Don't be fooled. The damage caused by lack of hope is insidious, and it is guaranteed to occur if you decide you deserve to take it easy and start to coast. Without active leadership, your business will begin to stall out.

You have to stay engaged and grow a little bit and keep everyone excited about the business. It's that excitement that causes people to get up early and put in all the discretionary effort the business must have to succeed. And your people are looking to you to provide it.

Without your consistent leadership, the business will begin to drift, and if it goes on long enough, one day you may find you've coasted right into bankruptcy.

◼ Trap 2:
I Don't Have to Learn Anything New

While building your business, you likely were active in both business development and personal development. You attended management and leadership training. You were young, hungry, and looking to improve.

Now that you've reached a certain level of success, you may think, "OK, my work is done. Thank goodness I don't have to go through all that training anymore! I'll leave that to my employees."

The only problem is it's not true!

No matter how big, bold, and wonderful your company becomes, your first job is *always* to grow yourself.

Remember, everyone in the business keys off you. And they key off your actions *today*, not your actions 10 years ago. If you are content with coasting and OK with personal stagnation, your employees will infer that is OK for them too. You are now asking them to do something you are not willing to do yourself, which is to improve every day.

Get some coaching. Keep going to leadership classes. Keep *growing*, because the minute you think "I've learned it all," you're already in trouble and starting to stagnate.

To keep it all going you have to keep investing in your own growth and you have to keep it up until the very end. Even if you only have a few years left before you plan to retire or pass on the company, you have to keep growing. Even if you've got leaders helping you, you're still the prime example of how people need to act.

This brings us to the third trap, which is thinking you're done with change and can rely on the status quo.

This Will Never Work (Don't Listen)
Tom Kelly

I am the son of a plumber. My father was a contractor. I worked for him and learned amazing lessons from him. My father was like many in this industry—he worked his whole life dedicated to this industry, his customers, and his employees.

I met Frank Blau Jr. and heard his message of pricing and professionalism in the mid-1980s. I remember my father stating firmly, "This will never work—flat-rate pricing just won't work." I respected my father, but saw the success Frank had created. In this regard, I chose to listen to Frank.

"When you are doing something different the first people who will tell you it is impossible are your competitors and industry associates. The last people you should emulate are your competitors, who are not living the kind of life you want to live."

Our friendship grew and I traveled with Frank when he was doing his "The Business of Contracting" seminars. I was his "bag boy," helping to set the room and otherwise keep Frank company on the road. I heard it a hundred times—"This will never work"—from longtime contractors in the room who were used to doing business a certain way. I chose not to listen to them either.

When Frank ran for Plumbing-Heating-Cooling Contractors Association (PHCC) president, I helped him campaign at the national convention in

New York City. Again, I heard it from leaders in the association: "This will never work—this college of business knowledge." Frank lost the election. Apparently, most of the conventioneers listened to the naysayers and "never weres." I didn't.

Finally, when Frank and George Brazil were talking about starting a new organization to bring the message forward, I went with Frank as he shared his vision with other contractors. Most people said, "This will never work. Contractors won't pay that kind of money for a membership."

In fact, prior to starting Nexstar we held a two-day informational meeting with a bunch of strong-willed contractors like Frank and George. We were talking about this idea of a new organization. What should it do? Who should run it? That kind of thing. We thought we were really smart and decided to hire an outside facilitator to keep us on track. One day in, after listening to us fight, the facilitator quit and gave us our money back. She said in disgust, "This will never work." I didn't listen to her either.

When you are doing something different the first people who will tell you it is impossible are your competitors and industry associates. The last people you should emulate are your competitors, who are not living the kind of life you want to live. The idea of Nexstar was heretical to longtime industry people. But once I decided how I wanted to live as a contractor, I knew we needed to create an organization that would help us get there. It was just that simple.

Know what you need in your own life and listen to the truly wise people who have created business success. We did, and Nexstar was created as a result.

■ Trap 3:
I Can Go with the Flow of the Status Quo

To grow to this size, at some point you had to accept that everything—your industry, your business, your customers, and, yes, even an employee or two—will be different in three months. Your ability to navigate and execute change in that dynamic workplace enabled you to grow.

Over time you implemented policies and procedures that determined what, when, and how things should be done. Your business is now running like a fine watch. You can take a week or two off to travel now and again without worrying.

The good news is the sum of all your decisions to date helped create your success. The bad news is, at this level, if you're too attached to the status quo you may find yourself in the change trap.

In business, there's no way around change—unless you want to stagnate. The trick is to *manage* it. And according to Peter Drucker, the renowned business author and strategist, "The most effective way to manage change is to create it."

In fact, if things have been going steady for a while, *you* should be the person to tip the table over—before an employee, customer, or competitor does it for you.

Why? Because change under duress stinks. When you have to change because you just lost three great technicians you will be reacting, and you will be reacting under stress. However, if *you* initiate the change, you are doing it on your own terms and on your own timetable.

The other facet of this trap has to do with the ability to change your mind in addition to the way you operate. This facet is when you become so resistant to new ideas that the business begins to lose energy and suffocate. One of the metaphors our (amazing) training group uses involves a simple furnace filter.

KEEPING YOUR FILTER CLEAN

The typical furnace filter is designed to protect the furnace. Its purpose is to keep the furnace from being damaged—not to make it more efficient.

Humans have a protective filter too. It's called our memory. Whenever we encounter a painful situation—say we touch a hot burner on the stove—we remember that pain and decide from that day forward to never knowingly touch a hot burner again. Our brain takes in information and then filters it through our experience to determine if it is good or bad for us.

Our memory filter is designed to protect us just like a furnace filter protects HVAC equipment. Our filter is *not* designed to help us thrive or be more efficient; it is designed to protect us from harm.

Eventually, we have a lifetime of experiences both good and bad, and those experiences collect in our filter, which is *supposed* to let the good in and stop the bad from getting in and hurting us.

The problem is sometimes our filter can become so clogged nothing at all can pass through—good or bad.

Eventually, this clogged filter, instead of protecting us, causes us harm. That's because it filters out *everything*, preventing fresh ideas from reaching our consciousness—just like a clogged furnace filter prevents fresh air from reaching the furnace.

To avoid this problem, our filter needs to be changed and cleaned as well, so new ideas can come through. You know your filter is clogged when you start to say things like:

"That won't work in my market."
"My customers are different."
"All customers want is the lowest price."
"All employees care about is their paycheck."

These are indications that your mind is closed to new opportunities.

The problem with this mind-set is it means the only changes you'll make will be forced, under duress, and in reaction to something bad happening.

You become vulnerable to this problem if you only take in information that reinforces your current state of being—for example, if you only read blogs and listen to TV news and podcasts that align with your existing point of view, or if you go to training seminars and only acknowledge the information that reinforces what you are doing while quickly dismissing the rest as inaccurate or unimportant.

I know it's comforting to take in information that reinforces your existing viewpoint. The danger is that you may start to immediately avoid or reject any information that conflicts with that point of view. This avoidance or rejection is especially harmful in business because it keeps out new ideas and concepts your business may need to succeed long term.

If this is happening to you, it means your filter is clogged. It needs cleaning!

As you age and have a measure of business success, you have to be especially vigilant about this trap. Make it a point to seek out new information and consider it thoughtfully. There is a huge difference between being wise and being close-minded!

Consider this industry prior to 1992. When Frank Blau Jr. introduced the concept of flat-rate pricing, young contractors who still had relatively clean filters jumped on the idea immediately and enjoyed business success. They were receptive to new ideas.

On the other hand, many tenured contractors who had operated for decades under time and materials pricing saw Frank as a heretic.

I often think back on why anyone would prefer time and materials over flat-rate pricing and I scratch my head. How could anyone defend it?

Frank was ridiculed for a long time by people in the industry who were completely closed off to new ideas about how to price their services. And they were bound and determined to defend their own viewpoint—at any cost.

Today, of course, you would be hard-pressed to find a residential service company that operated on time and materials. What was once viewed as heretical is now the industry standard.

So, check yourself. If you are saying dangerous things like, "That will never work in my market," it is time to check and clean your filter so you don't accidentally filter out the new ideas you need to keep your business fresh. ▪

CHAPTER

14

BUILDING LEADERS

Leadership is not easy. It can be lonely. It often involves conflict and making hard decisions. That's why it's your responsibility to provide your leadership team with the continuous mentoring required to ensure they think like you do.

It's not enough to make sure your leaders are engaged. That's table stakes. You also have to make sure they are properly indoctrinated with your business philosophy and master plan. Otherwise your business may struggle or even decline.

■ Shaping the Thinking

As the owner of your company, it's your responsibility to invest the time to shape the thinking of your leaders so you can feel confident that they would make decisions similar to those you would make given most circumstances. Your goal really is to equip them to make even better decisions than you would make!

When Nexstar was founded, Frank Blau Jr. spent hours on the phone with me. Frank knew the kind of organization he wanted to build and what we needed to do. It would have been very easy for him (in the short term) to just tell me what to do. But he didn't. Instead, Frank mentored me. He taught me how to think about the business rather than prescribing my every move.

Here is what Frank did: He sent me a business article to read. Then he called and asked me what I took from the article, and we discussed my take-aways. In this way, Frank helped develop my thinking. He didn't want to direct Nexstar from Milwaukee or anyplace else. He had to trust me to make good decisions and he knew the only way that was going to happen was if he trained me how to think like he did.

I spent hundreds of hours on the phone with Frank, at all hours, discussing not only *what* we should do but also *why* we should do certain things. At the time, I was not fully aware of Frank's motives. I thought he was just interested in Nexstar and maybe a little bit bored.

Upon reflection (years later), I realized that Frank was shaping me as a thought leader. He was making sure I was equipped to make decisions that were aligned with the best interests of Nexstar. It was an enormous time commitment for Frank to spend hours on the phone with a young, dumb kid. But he did, and thank you Frank!

Have you invested time in shaping the thinking of your leaders so they will lead like you would, in the same way Frank did for me?

You won't be a true master until you do.

■ Why You Are Different and What You Are Building

As part of the mentoring process, you need to make sure all leaders in your company understand, own, and can articulate on demand why your company is different and what it is you are building.

"Why you are different" is your mission. It's why you exist. It's the thing that is special and different about your business that sets it apart from the 80,000 other PHCE companies in North America.

Here at Nexstar our mission is to guide and develop the independent service provider to be simply the best in customer service, profitability, and employee engagement.

That is what we do and who we endeavor to be as an organization. And this mission has been essentially the same for the past 25 years.

Your vision is what you are building together. It's your conception of what success will look like when the mission is being fulfilled. It's a quantifiable description of the business at some point in the future.

Here at Nexstar we have cast a vision that is all about the success of our members. By 2022, the median Nexstar member will have 10 percent revenue

Naysayers and Finger-Pointers

Jim Hamilton

When I started my service business in 1990 in Kansas City, I was the only contractor providing a flat-rate pricing structure to customers. The competition all stated I'd be out of business in three months. I remember showing off my two trucks at the local Plumbing-Heating-Cooling Contractors Association (PHCC) meeting. Every contractor at that meeting said, "You're a crook. You'll be out of business in three months. Your customers will never call you back after you've screwed them. Your customers will never buy from you again. Your prices are too high. You don't know what you're doing." They were so sure of their advice for me.

I didn't listen to them. I knew I was right. I knew these guys were among the 50 contractors I was with in Wichita, Kansas, when I first learned how to sell at the right price at Frank's seminar. They all had the wrong price then, and they still all had the wrong price! I was the only contractor in town who had the right price. I knew what I saw when I visited Frank's shop, and I believed what Frank showed me. That was my focus.

As time went on, those same contractors who had given me advice started trying to figure out what I was doing.

Looking back at it today—at the naysayers and the finger-pointers—I never gave it a thought. I didn't care what losers thought; I only cared about doing what was right for me and my family. I knew that Frank's influence was improving my business, and competitors were wondering how I did it. In 1990, I was the only contractor providing an upfront pricing structure, most commonly called flat rate. And now, fast-forward to 2017, I don't know of any contractor in town still charging time and materials. Everyone has switched over to an upfront pricing method. The model I was using was destined to put me out of business if I had listened to my competitors in 1990. Today it is a standard business practice.

growth and 15 percent net profitability. That's it. Simple to understand, and because it's measurable, it will be easy to tell when we've achieved it.

That is what we are building here at Nexstar. It's what success will look like when our mission has been accomplished. Our leaders understand it, own it, and can recite it upon demand. They also understand that all actions taken should be moving us closer to the fulfillment of this vision.

Having a compelling mission and vision is vital to creating an engaged leadership team. It shows that the business is about more than you, the owner. It also enables all leaders to align with a common purpose and goal.

But wait, there's more! In addition to aligning with your mission and vision, leaders must also align with a set of guiding principles that clearly articulate the values of your company.

■ Guiding Principles

What is right and wrong? What is appropriate behavior? How should we treat each other? And the $1 million question: What framework can employees rely on to make good decisions without asking for help?

You need guiding principles exactly because the impact of the answers to these questions gets magnified as a business grows at the master level.

Without guiding principles in place, you may end up with six different managers and six different ideas of what is right or wrong, what is correct or incorrect behavior, and how employees should be treated.

Frankly, this is where a lot of companies fall apart. Managers start to act on their own accord, divisions in the company start to appear, and these divisions will tear your company apart if left unchecked.

Here at Nexstar, we have six principles that guide our thinking. These principles help us make decisions that are uniform and aligned with our mission and vision. They also enable staff to work through sticky situations without having to ask me or another senior leader for counsel. Here they are:

1 • M-1 (Members First)

2 • Bad News Early, Good News Often

3 • See It, Say It—Directly and with Respect

4 • Live Business Excellence as We Teach Business Excellence

5 • Bring More Energy to Work Than You Take

6 • Culture of Caring, but Not Enabling

I personally walk every new employee through each of these principles and explain what they mean and how they can use them in their job.

Occasionally, during a monthly staff meeting, we also ask an employee to take one and expound on it and how it shapes their thinking. And perhaps most importantly, during weekly one-on-ones, supervisors and employees discuss actions taken that were aligned or unaligned with these principles.

This is thought leadership development. This process helps leaders who are managing your good people learn to think in a way that is consistent across the business and in alignment with your thinking.

Just like Frank did for me.

As your business grows, this strategic work will become increasingly important. Maybe you didn't need it to get where you are, but as a master with a business that's growing in size and complexity daily, you need it now more than ever. ■

LEADERSHIP WISDOM

■ Endless Patience

One time I was relaying a story to Frank Blau Jr. about a member who had been struggling for an extended period of time. The member was just difficult. He seemed to be unwilling to, as Frank would say, "take the medicine." I mean, this went on for *years.*

At Nexstar it is rare that we "fire" a member. It happens, but if a member is engaged and trying we will continue to work with them. But the word around the office for this member was that there was not much hope of success.

However, after years of effort on Nexstar's behalf, the member began to make positive moves. His business, while not a high flyer, was improving and going in the right direction. The owner was less of a know-it-all and more receptive to coaching and support. I was very surprised and told Frank as much.

Frank, at age 85, reminded me that with members I have to have "endless patience." He said, "Don't give up, Jack. You never know when they will take the medicine." I reflected on this message and my earlier cynicism.

When you run a business for an extended period of time, it is easy to become cynical. The harsh reality is the turnaround that happened with this member is not common. Most of the time members and employees who are struggling don't ever "get it." The challenging employees remain challenging despite our best efforts. And in the end, we usually ask them to leave the company or, in Nexstar's case, the member eventually quits.

After so many years in business, you may get tired of the same complaints from employees. You don't want to hear it anymore. You start to tell yourself the story that "people can't change" or "no matter what I do the employees won't appreciate it."

This is dangerous head trash because what happens next is you are the one who kind of quits.

When you're younger, you don't know you can't do something so you try. And while you don't change everyone, you do indeed make a difference—even if it is small. You're happy with any incremental improvement.

As time goes on, it's easy to lose sight of this. You may begin to focus on those people who did not change or on the few that lied, cheated, and took advantage of you. Left unchecked, these negative thoughts may start to consume all of your attention. You may become so sick of it all that you'll stop trying to manage through it and won't do anything to fix it or make it better.

Frank reminded me that there is always hope and that you should always keep trying. His optimism belies his age. Frank is young at heart and that's what you need when it comes to people development.

You've got to keep trying! Keep young people coming into the business because they don't have this cynicism. They are idealistic. They bring new problems, of course, but also new energy to make things better.

You may never solve a specific problem, but if you keep going you will help people. Frank never lost his optimism about changing people and that is a good lesson for all of us.

Keep trying. You can make a difference even if it is just a small change and even if you don't believe your efforts will be fully rewarded. Keep trying!

What's a higher use of business than helping people? There's wealth building, but at this point we have wealth. Business becomes a vehicle to change lives for the better—yours and theirs.

Keep that at the front of your mind so when you have bad days, and feel sick of doing this, your passion for the business and the people in it can be rekindled.

What you focus on you will find. Learn from the failures, but remember the successes and derive energy from those experiences.

■ Don't Fall in Love with Nothing That Can't Love You Back

"Don't fall in love with nothing that can't love you back" is an actual quote from a lifelong friend. It was initially voiced as a reminder to not stick with a stock market investment for too long—something I had recently done. But this advice applies to business initiatives as well.

It means don't hold onto things or people that are holding the business—and everyone who is working hard in it—back.

If you are like me, you have had great ideas that you have lots of passion about that you have undertaken. When it is your idea and you initiate it, you have ownership and pride. You can fall in love with a business initiative and defend it for no other reason than it was your idea. And as the Good Book says, "Pride goeth before a fall."

It is very easy to lose your objectivity when it is your idea. Taken further, it is especially easy to lose objectivity when a change will cause more work for you personally.

As your business grows, its needs to change—not only *what* it needs to be successful, but also *who* it needs. Let's talk about who first.

If you're like most owners we know, you will wake up one day and realize there is an employee who is holding the company back. And let me tell you, if you hired the person or if firing them will result in more work for you, it is likely that you are the last person in your business who has come to this realization.

This happens for any number of reasons. You might have inadvertently promoted them past their ability or things may have changed in their life so they no longer have the capacity to perform at the required level. Maybe there was a divorce or an illness—or maybe their "why" has been lost or changed and no longer aligns with your company's mission and vision.

This is a painful realization. You are in love with the idea of this person finishing their career at your company. It's only a few years away after all! Or, you know if this person is let go, the work they are doing will fall on you for a while.

But in the meantime things are falling apart. Goals are not being met. And other employees are having to work harder to cover for this person. It's a dilemma: if you take action it will negatively impact the employee and maybe you, but if you delay it will continue to harm the rest of the employees.

TOUGH DECISIONS ENSURE THE FUTURE OF THE MAJORITY

This is tough stuff, but as a leader entrusted with the financial future of others, it is one of the decisions you will likely have to make. And this does not get easier as the business grows; it gets *harder*.

In his book *Traction: Get a Grip on Your Business*, author Gino Wickman recommends reviewing employees against three key questions:

1 • Are they able/capable? Do they have the expertise and experience required?

2 • Are they willing?

3 • Do they have the capacity?

Sometimes people have the ability and willingness but over time lose the *capacity* to do the job.

Maybe their life circumstances have shifted so they have to leave early several days a week. Or maybe there has been a change in their physical capabilities where they can't effectively work a full eight-hour day without extreme fatigue. You want it for them, but they just can't do it anymore.

This also happens to owners, by the way. You may have the ability and willingness to run a great business, but if you don't have the *capacity*—meaning the health, energy, and circumstances—anymore, you may need to concede that you are the problem!

The other area where people get caught is in adding new service lines. It's easy to fall totally in love with an idea because it's something new and exciting. Since it's your idea, you defend it ferociously, even if it is clearly destroying value in the business.

I can clearly recall working with a Nexstar member while I was a business coach. He asked me to come to his shop to help him figure out how to "make more money." He claimed the overall business was in a tough spot. After reviewing his P/L and balance sheet, I could not have agreed more. The business was

Taking the Medicine
Brad Martin

Life is full of opportunities. Sometimes you have to grab them, and sometimes you are lucky enough that they grab you as they go by.

In the fall of 1992, I read an article in *PM Magazine* about a new organization that was forming to improve the mechanical service industry. I made a call to a young man in Minneapolis named Jack Tester who was the executive director of Contractors 2000. He explained the new group. He also told me it cost $4,000 to join. Wow! I signed a check and mailed it off to Minneapolis. (I hid the check from my dad, who had started the company.)

I knew I needed guidance to improve my business. I had done all I knew to do. I hoped that Contractors 2000 would give me a new start. My service manager Jim Craig and I booked flights to Anaheim, California, to attend the first Contractors 2000 Super Meeting.

We toured two of George Brazil's shops and sat in meetings for two days. I also got to meet Frank Blau Jr.; it was his birthday. The organization was in its infancy and it really had nothing to offer except the opportunity to talk to like-minded contractors from all over the country.

> *"I knew I needed guidance to improve my business. I had done all I knew to do."*

Though we were all in the same industry, we all did business a little differently. Some companies were good at marketing, some were good at operations, and others were good at customer service. We all learned from each other. Jim and I went home with a list of 200 items that we wanted to implement in our company as soon as possible. It was the guidance we needed to take our company beyond the next level and into the future.

My opportunity came when I was elected to the board of directors. I had the privilege to serve on the board with the giants of the industry, which included Frank and George. As a 38-year-old who had just become president of a small company in Amarillo, Texas, I had the opportunity to get to know and learn from the best.

"I was lucky enough to stand on the shoulders of giants to grow my business."

Our company began to grow and prosper because we "took the medicine," as Frank would say. Later, as chairman of Contractors 2000, I had the opportunity to work with the board of directors, Jack Tester, and many new friends to lay the foundation of Contractors 2000.

We attended Super Meetings (three per year at the time) religiously. Early on, each member would bring their service tickets, brochures, yellow page ads, and more and throw them on the tables for all to see. Each member took copies of what they thought their companies needed. We all grew and became better business people because we were willing to share and educate each other.

I was lucky enough to stand on the shoulders of giants to grow my business. I could not have done it without Nexstar and its extraordinary members. I sold Scottco when I was 53 years old and have been pursuing my dreams ever since, which included becoming a Nexstar business coach.

hemorrhaging cash and was mere months from insolvency. While reviewing his P/L, the numbers right in front of me showed that his electrical service line was losing money *on the gross profit line*. He actually had a *negative* gross profit in electrical service. I had never seen a service line with such poor performance.

It was very clear that this strong plumbing company was being eaten alive by a relatively new service line that was being grossly mismanaged. It was also clear to me that a good plan to turn it around would have to come from outside the company with a new manager—a big and risky task.

This was a firefight kind of consulting trip. We had to figure out how to make the company profitable—and quick—or in a year his bank would be presiding over a bankruptcy sale. As an outsider, it was clear to me that a relatively easy answer would be to shut down the electrical service line. That would be much easier than taking the owner's attention away from plumbing, which was highly profitable, or finding a white knight electrical manager from outside the company in the next few weeks.

I was objective. I did not make the decision to add electrical to this company. I had not hired any of the people or made a single decision that contributed to the failure of this department. Rarely in business has a decision been so easy to make. To me, shuttering the electrical service line was a complete no-brainer.

However, when I made this strong recommendation to the owner he would not do it. He did not want to admit defeat. He was in love with the idea of being a multi-trade contractor even though this decision was costing him hundreds of thousands of dollars a year and risking his life's work. This is an extreme example, but it is illustrative of the pride that can harm an otherwise successful business—especially if it has been successful for quite a while.

When something is destroying your business, if you aren't in love with it, it's easy to kill it. When you fall in love with an idea, and it doesn't work, you're more likely to defend it past the point of reason.

Be objective with people and business ventures, especially when it comes to your own decisions.

If something is hurting the business, costing you money, and is not grounded in your long-term plan, shut it down or get rid of it. Don't fall in love with nothing that can't love you back.

■ Got Communication Rhythms?

At the master level, you are no longer involved in everything and you are not directly involved with employees anymore either. Responsibility for the company is now spread across roles, and those individuals in charge of the different pieces of the business need autonomy.

What naturally happens as a business becomes decentralized is individual managers will make decisions, and those decisions will have some impact on others *outside* of their department or function.

It might have been a good decision, but since you or one of your managers made it without getting others' input, some may end up feeling hurt, confused, or just out of the loop. For many this can also be demotivating.

If you employ a "knowing" person, meaning they have to be involved in everything all the time, they are going to struggle as your business gets bigger. You will have to work extra hard to help this person understand the impossibility of keeping everyone apprised of every decision. If they can't accept this, a larger, decentralized business may not be the right environment for them. In a big business, this is just life!

To reduce this friction, however, it's your job to make sure that clear "communication rhythms" are in place.

Communication rhythms are recurring meetings with specific agendas designed to increase awareness, support teamwork and collaboration, and reduce lack of communication, fostering trust across the company.

SILOS HAPPEN

As different people start to own parts of the business, silos will happen. Your communication rhythms are what will make those silos not quite as tall and impenetrable. Essential meetings include:

- ■ A 10-minute daily huddle where the day's activities are planned.

- ■ Weekly 30-minute supervisor-to-employee one-on-ones where a specific sequence of questions is answered and support is provided. This ensures all employees have an opportunity to clear up misunderstandings and understand clearly what is expected of them.

■ Weekly managers' meeting where progress against goals is measured and issues are processed.

These are the essential communication rhythms. If you become good at these meetings and hold them consistently, you will break down many of the barriers and silos that naturally occur in larger businesses.

Communication rhythms do not *eliminate* lack of communication—that's impossible—but they go a long way toward making sure communications across your company are as good as they can possibly be.

At Nexstar, we use a great format for weekly meetings called Level 10 Meetings. This format is described in detail in Gino Wickman's book *Traction*.

IT WILL NEVER BE PERFECT

Communications in your big business will never be perfect. There will always be something that wasn't fully communicated or discussed. It will never be totally fixed or done. When your business is this large and complex there will also be some silos between departments, some tension between employees, and some information that should have been shared but was forgotten.

This is just the tension that comes with having a bigger business. To eliminate it, you would have to shrink. The only thing you can do is improve communication rhythms and accept that there will always be some conflict.

Some days will seem perfectly harmonious, but then there will be other days where you forget to tell someone something and they get upset or think you're out to get them. Remember, this is the life you chose, the conflict you chose. You started with the conflict that comes with being small with only one truck; now you no longer have that conflict.

There are things that occur as you scale up a business that you just have to reconcile. New problems emerge as old ones go away. Just keep focused on the benefit of the new situation as you wrangle the new problems.

UNCONSCIOUS COMPETENCE

The good news is as you grow by solving new problems and learning how to communicate, these rhythms will become second nature. All your experiences will accumulate and you'll acquire an unconscious competence. When your communication rhythms are in place, and your mission, vision, and guiding principles are clear, the whole organization develops this unconscious competence. People will begin to do the right things without effort.

This realization will come to you one day. You will realize you have built an amazing company that is operating in concert at a high level, like an orchestra.

And that is a beautiful thing. ■

GIANT

BIG SHOULDERS

GIANT

You've decided how you really want to live and you've learned how to change your business to begin moving toward that vision (Section 1: Apprentice). You now also understand how to grow the business and your people so you can secure your future (Section 2: Journeyman). You are aware that it's no longer about your success only—it's about using what you've created and everything you've learned to help others become effective leaders (Section 3: Master).

Central to this advanced mission is challenging your management team to learn how to think the way you would think. This mentoring is essential because it will enable those managers to make decisions that are as good as (or better than) yours. It also will ensure that their decisions will be in alignment with your vision so the company continues to grow and thrive, and everyone associated with it has the chance to live the way they want to live too.

It's only when you are doing all of these things successfully that the next and final level—giant—becomes accessible.

You have to create leaders who are capable of passing on your wisdom to others, who will then create even more leaders.

When you have created a business full of amazing people who are willing and able to pass on all they've learned to others, you have become a giant.

16

BIG SHOULDERS

At the master level, it's no longer about your success only. It's about using what you've created and all that you've learned to help others become effective leaders. It's about becoming a giant. A giant kneels down and lets others climb up on their shoulders. He or she is fulfilled by lifting others up so they can see for the first time what is *possible*.

■ Three Keys

Giants are essentially mentor coaches who provide leaders with three main things: vision, stability, and influence.

VISION

As a giant, you provide leaders with a clear vision of a future state of being for their business and for their own abilities, which they don't yet perceive to be possible.

You communicate this vision to your future leaders and provide them with a series of specific goals that once achieved you know will make that vision a reality.

STABILITY

Giants possess physical, mental, and emotional strength and character. They are also financially stable. As a giant, you are a leader whom people can lean on and learn from. You model consistency and you are always present and available. You walk your talk.

INFLUENCE

Giants influence and develop leaders, who will then go on to influence and develop other leaders, who will ultimately repeat the process, influencing and developing still other leaders. This expands your reach to people you will never meet, helping them live the way they want to live.

As a giant, you focus your attention on taking action that ultimately will have a far-ranging, even exponential, positive impact on current and future generations.

■ Cascading Effect

Because of Frank Blau Jr. and, by extension, Nexstar, people have been empowered to change their lives—starting with the lives of people who knew Frank personally and then over the years extending to others who had never heard of him or Nexstar.

Frank said it was his mother who emphasized the advice that if he learned anything that would benefit his fellow man, he must share it so the next generation would have it better than the last. She was a giant in Frank's life.

So when Frank became a contractor, and discovered the great shortcomings within an industry he said was operating "almost like in the dark ages," he decided to do something about it.

Through his relentless efforts educating contractors and advocating for them, Frank helped others make the decision to change their lives.

Frank didn't change their lives. They did. But it was Frank's vision, stability, and influence that allowed them to accomplish great things for themselves.

Frank knew he needed a structure where those he trained could then turn around and train others. As a result, he created Nexstar.

■ The Original Industry Giant

Frank Blau Jr. is the original industry giant. Haunted by his mother's words, Frank took action, and his efforts have already impacted multiple generations.

Here's how Frank's impact on just one person has cascaded through generations of industry leaders, starting with Nexstar business coach Jim Hamilton.

Jim attended one of Frank's "The Business of Contracting" seminars in 1990. Jim was a struggling new-construction plumbing contractor in Kansas City, living day to day like virtually every other contractor at the time.

Jim recalled, "I met Frank and I sat in that seminar and said, 'I can do this.' The next thing I knew, I was up at Frank's place in Wisconsin, and he was showing me everything about this business. It absolutely changed my life."

As a result, Jim created a very successful business that he ultimately sold. He now gives back to the industry as a Nexstar business coach.

When John Conway joined Nexstar in 2004, his Memphis-based HVAC company was almost a million dollars in debt. Then, Jim Hamilton became John's Nexstar business coach.

John said, "Jim showed me a way and gave me a vision. He helped me establish what my goals should be on a daily, weekly, and monthly basis. I was then able to pass those goals on to my key managers and my frontline employees. We then attacked the business daily to meet those goals. Five years after joining Nexstar, I was debt-free. I didn't owe anybody a dime. It happened because of the vision Jim gave me, one I couldn't have seen before I met him. Jim is the reason I'm the leader I am today."

Jim Hamilton took what he learned from Frank Blau Jr. and passed it on to John Conway.

Jim Hamilton is a giant.

John Conway ultimately sold his company and now also gives back to the industry as a Nexstar business coach.

While still working in his business in 2007, John Conway met a young woman while buying a personal cell phone from a Verizon store. He was so impressed by her customer service skills that he recruited her into his business.

Tracy Robinson was promoted through Conway Services, taking on increasing levels of responsibility and growing as a leader.

Tracy said, "There are a few lessons I learned from John that really stand out. First, to succeed, each person has to understand what their individual goal is and how they play into the overall company's success. It's my job to communicate that effectively. Once people are empowered to take control of their own destiny, there is no stopping them!

"Second, I learned it's great to have a plan, and sometimes it's great to have a backup plan. But more important is taking action. John said, 'Hard work wins when wishing won't.' It means I can't just wish away my goals; I have to take action to achieve them.

"Finally, John taught me to surround myself with people who inspire excellence in others, and that's exactly what I found in the Nexstar Network family."

Jim Hamilton passed on what he learned from Frank Blau Jr. to John Conway, and John Conway passed it on to Tracy Robinson.

John Conway is a giant.

Tracy now works for Nexstar as a call center coach, giving back to the industry by developing leaders in call center and dispatch functions.

Now, in 2017, Tracy Robinson is coaching Allison Minda, who is the call center manager for Nexstar member company PK Wadsworth Heating and Cooling in Ohio.

Allison said, "While I've been in leadership roles before, Tracy has really helped me claim ownership of those leadership qualities and make the most of them. One of the most profound gifts she has given me is permission to be myself in a professional environment. She has shown me that I can communicate serious directions and expectations *and* bring a sense of levity and fun into the office every day. And our numbers just keep getting better! Her processes and methods are not solving life's great mysteries, but the way in which she transmits them—and in turn teaches me to do the same with my team—makes every day feel less like a 'have to' and more like a 'get to.'"

Tracy learned from John Conway, and passed on what she learned to Allison.

Tracy Robinson is a giant.

And since Allison is training her staff with the knowledge and wisdom she has learned from Tracy, she is on her way to becoming a giant, too.

Allison has never met Frank, or Jim, or John. But because she is now standing on Tracy's shoulders, and Tracy is standing on all of theirs, they all have in some way contributed to her success.

I Had Nothing to Lose So I Jumped Right In

Dan Weltman

In 1991, the Gulf War recession was in full swing and things were bad, both in the world's economy and in our little plumbing company. Then, in November, my service truck was stolen out of my driveway. It eventually was found—stripped of all tools and equipment, devastating me both financially and emotionally. In December, I had to loan personal money to the company to clear payroll Christmas week.

Around that same time, I read about a plumbing contractor who was touring the country giving a seminar called "The Business of Contracting." Frank Blau Jr. had plenty of these seminars scheduled, but I was always too busy to attend because my father had retired in late 1991 and now I was running the company. There was no way I could leave to attend a seminar. Who would answer the phones? Who would order the materials and pay the bills? No one else could do that job in our four-person company.

Also bear in mind that at this point in my life, I worked 51 weeks, waiting for my tax refund check to arrive. Once it did, I drove to my brother-in-law's house in Florida for Easter week. This went on for years!

By divine intervention, I ended up attending my first Blau seminar on January 30, 1992. My parents had decided to return three days early from vacation, which was one day before the conference! Pop came into our little office and took over the phone duties, and I ended up registering at the conference room door minutes before the seminar started.

Frank was simultaneously amazing and intimidating. He told us we were the world's best technicians because we could fix anything. He also told us we were the world's worst businessmen because we didn't understand basic markup principles and didn't realize that profit dollars were derived from overhead.

I walked out of the seminar with my head spinning and spent the next couple days diving into my checkbook receipts and invoices.

We weren't charging enough money for our services. Sold hours? Overhead? Billable hour efficiency? These words were foreign to me.

The selling price I developed that weekend scared me, but with some faith (and more than a little desperation) we put flat-rate pricing into effect on Monday, February 3, 1992—and it worked.

I started corresponding with Frank and we exchanged a few phone calls. He would always call me back, no matter where he was in the country or what day of the week it was. This man from Milwaukee, who was fast becoming a good friend, would do anything to help me, which speaks volumes to who Frank really is.

Per our family tradition, in April of 1992 I cashed my tax refund check and headed to my brother-in-law's place in Ft. Lauderdale. Coincidentally, Frank was giving a seminar at a nearby hotel. I popped in unannounced with my then three-year-old daughter asleep on my shoulder. Frank asked me to speak to the class about my experience implementing his system.

Then, in August, Frank called and asked me to join him at his place for a "meeting of the minds." He was forming a "college of knowledge" called Contractors 2000. With some trepidation, I wrote a check for $3,000, and found myself on the inaugural board of directors.

Since that fateful year, the application of all that I have learned from Frank and through Nexstar has allowed me to create a life that has taken me to places I never imagined possible a quarter century ago. I have financial security for myself, my wife, my children, and now my grandson. And I have a network of amazing friends around this great country of ours.

Reflecting on 25 years of Nexstar membership, I consider my association with this group as a meaningful and powerful part of my life—right up there with meeting and marrying my wife and the birth of my children.

Sharing knowledge, ambitions, dreams, and goals over the years with the likes of Frank Blau, George Brazil, Jack Tester, Tom Kelly, Jim Hamilton, and the membership at large has created a lifelong unbreakable bond. And Contractors 2000—now Nexstar—helped define who I am not just as a business professional, but also as a husband, father, brother, sibling, and grandfather. I look forward to drinking from its well of wisdom for a long time to come.

What Is Your Goal Today?

John Conway

I remember it like it was yesterday. I had invited my business coach Jim Hamilton for an on-site visit to my shop in January of 2006. During his first morning at my shop, Jim spent his time with my key employees. He asked them three questions:

1. What is your goal today?
2. What is the company goal today?
3. How do you contribute to the company goal?

I was floored. Not one of my employees could answer those questions. And then Jim asked me the same three questions. That's where the trouble really started, because I couldn't answer the questions either! Probably the same reason none of my employees knew the company goal.

If no one in the business knows the company goal (including the owner), it is not possible to achieve the company goal.

You see, every company has a company goal even if no one working there knows what it is. Every company requires a certain amount of revenue and gross profit daily to survive. The company (as an entity) doesn't care if you don't know or achieve the goal because the mailman continues to bring the bills.

To succeed, do the following:

1. Establish and know your company goal daily.
2. Communicate your goal.
3. Track progress to your goal daily.
4. Achieve your company goal.

PAYING IT FORWARD

As a giant, you're always paying it forward to the next generation so they can have it better than the last. You give without expecting anything in return because someone was thoughtful and kind enough to do the same for you.

You accepted that gift, made it better, and now it's time to pass it on so others may have the opportunity to live the way they really want and deserve to live.

It all started with two men, Frank Blau Jr. and George Brazil, who felt compelled to pass on the success principles they'd learned to others doing the same job—and thank God they did! They created Nexstar to make sure the knowledge they'd fought so hard to acquire could continue to help others learn how to change their lives, long after they had concluded their careers.

At some point, your career as a business owner will conclude, too. When you look back on it, what will you see? When you compare the money you've made to the lives you have helped change, which will you be most proud of? What will stick with you as you reflect on your accomplishments and career?

Will it be the young people you helped? Those who wandered in and joined you without a set direction and with your guidance (or guidance from one of your leaders) created a purposeful career that is now part of their identity and something they can be proud of?

Or are you still operating from a position of scarcity, hoarding your knowledge, and believing that giving anything away means less for you, instead of more?

We hope this isn't the case.

Why? Because passing on what you learned to people who will teach it to others is the highest use of your efforts. The positive impact you have on people's lives is the thing you'll remember and the thing that will live beyond you and your business, and it will mean more to you than your paycheck or investment portfolio ever will.

When giants step forward and allow others to climb up onto their shoulders and see beyond their limited beliefs and fears to what is possible, *amazing* things happen.

THE ULTIMATE GOAL

The ultimate goal is to pass on all this hard-won knowledge and wisdom to others, with the expectation that they should pay it forward and pass their knowledge on to someone else so that future generations can have it better than the last. And all can live the way they really want to live.

We hope you'll pay it forward by allowing others to stand on your shoulders, see what's possible, and learn from your example.

You can do this—all of it.

You might not believe it right now. But we do. We know it is possible because we see it every day. We have members that have built and sold multimillion-dollar businesses in a lot fewer than 25 years. They did it using the principles in this book, and you can do it, too.

Wherever you are on the journey, begin now. Claim the right to live the way you want to live and take the steps to bring it to reality. It will be challenging sometimes, and there always will be some conflict, but your commitment to being extraordinary and following these principles will pay off.

You can do it and you are worth it. ■

EPILOGUE: THE FRANK BLAU JR. STORY

Frank J. Blau Jr. began as a plumbing apprentice in 1951 and achieved journeyman status in 1955. It wasn't long, however, before Frank realized that even with incremental raises and journeyman status his earnings were not going to keep pace with the needs of his growing family, much less allow him to live the way he really wanted to live. So, in 1960, with just $600 in working capital, Frank started Blau Plumbing.

One of the first things Frank did as a new business owner was join the Milwaukee Plumbing Contractors Association (MPCA) because he thought it would be a source of business knowledge. Unfortunately, Frank soon discovered it was mostly a social club. Industry associations at the time were focused primarily on technical, political issues and socializing. In fact, when it came to making money in the plumbing business, Frank realized no one in the industry knew anything! Hungry for this information, Frank set about educating himself.

An article on markup and margin in *Domestic Engineering* magazine changed everything for Frank. He recalled, "The markup and margin concept was so foreign to me at first that I read the article three times. But once I got it, I finally knew what I was doing wrong when estimating my work." Frank was giving away profit dollars due to a simple math mistake he was making when creating estimates.

At the time, Blau Plumbing was doing only new construction work. When he told his construction builders he needed to raise his prices, many derided him. "We'll replace you in a heartbeat!" they said. And many did just that.

But Frank knew that if he was going to live the way he wanted to live, his prices had to increase. The problem was he was competing against people who were not professionals, and as a result their prices were too low to make a profit. If he was going to make more money, Frank realized he would have to educate his competitors on what they needed to be charging. He began teaching a business management course at the Milwaukee Plumbing-Heating-Cooling Contractors Association (MPHCCA). He also pushed the state contractor's association to work with the Wisconsin licensing board to make business courses compulsory for the master plumber examination. During this time, Frank also undertook many personal efforts to improve the public image of the plumbing industry. At an early age, Frank was trying to change the industry.

Frank exited the new-construction industry abruptly in 1971, after he discovered his jobsite foreman playing cards and drinking beer instead of working at a large church project. This was the tipping point. He had finally had it with low-bid new-construction work. He called his brother Eddie and told him, "We're going full bore into service, and you're going to be our marketing guy."

Frank and Eddie were advertising pioneers. Blau Plumbing was one of the first contracting companies to recognize the power of primary yellow page position, and they ran full-page ads in the yellow pages. They purchased large panel trucks and made them into rolling billboards by plastering them with their distinctive logo and bright red, white, and blue graphics.

Blau Plumbing's company headquarters fronted a busy highway, and zoning did not allow for billboards. Functioning cranes, however, were considered part of the business so Eddie erected an old crane with the company logo at the top, further branding their business to thousands of Milwaukee residents each day. This seems normal today, but it was avant-garde marketing at the time.

Frank also was the first to give his technicians handheld computers, and introduced company-branded shut-off valve tags to the industry, among other things.

Frank's greatest innovation, however, was his belief that hardworking contractors should be rewarded for their efforts. Not only the business owners, but also the employees that helped those owners earn their wealth.

Frank paid his people well, gave them and their families health insurance, and provided lucrative profit sharing and fully funded retirement plans. If an employee was to give Blau Plumbing 20 to 25 years of service, Frank wanted him or her to be able to retire in comfort. Frank's motives came from the heart. He chokes up with pride and satisfaction when he talks about the wealth his employees managed to accumulate through his company.

Frank's initial motivation to figure out how to be a successful business-man was based on selfish reasons—he needed to provide for his large family. But Frank had three close calls with death that shifted his point of view forever. He realized that there was a reason he was still alive and that changing this industry was that reason. Frank truly believed his life's calling was to change the PHCE industry.

The Business of Contracting

Frank's seminar, "The Business of Contracting," continued to grow in popular-ity, and by the mid-1980s, in addition to leading Blau Plumbing, Frank traveled the country teaching, mentoring, and, in some cases, demanding contractors "take the medicine" by charging the right price.

Frank never expected anyone to take what he said at face value, and so to prove to people that they could trust what he said, he showed his personal W-2s at the beginning of the seminar. He said, "Here's the proof, and you can do it too." Many thought this was just an ego trip for Frank. That was not the case. Frank wanted people to know that he had lived what he was teaching, and he was proof of the success that can come if you "take the medicine."

You see, Frank hated false prophets, having seen the havoc they had cre-ated in the industry. Many of these men—despite their own business failures—had risen to positions of influence through trade associations. Frank believed you needed to live the principles you were teaching and be the example first before you could tell others what to do. It was sound advice then and remains sound advice now. In fact, in order to qualify to serve on the Nexstar board you must submit financial information on the company you own proving business success. It is a bylaws requirement that Frank instituted on day one at Nexstar.

Unfortunately, many in the industry objected to Frank's advice, and his direct confrontational approach made some others feel threatened. Many people not only resisted the message but also actively campaigned against it! It is safe to say Frank had many admirers, but he created many enemies as well. Pioneers always take the arrows, and Frank will confess many of them found his backside as he was traveling the country confronting business ignorance. However, those who did "take the medicine" saw their businesses change immediately for the better.

In 1995, Frank handed off management of Blau Plumbing to his sons, and the year 2000 marked his official retirement. Most people this successful would have hung it up and gone fishing, but not Frank. Instead, he redoubled his efforts to educate anyone in the industry who would listen on the business of contracting.

To this end, Frank wrote two columns for *PM Magazine* (1985–2003) dedicated to educating, inspiring, and providing hope and a way to a better life for thousands of fellow contractors. One column titled "How Much Should a Contractor Charge?" attacked the "going rate" as the ethical rate in this industry. This article was the turning point for many contractors who embraced it as the plumbing industry's own declaration of independence.

Though his focus was on crunching the numbers, Frank's influence went far beyond that. Jim Olystinski, then publisher of *PM Magazine*, said, "Frank was a blue-collar philosopher, someone who not only knew numbers and had a mission but also was a class warrior in the best sense of the word. Every column had the same underlying message, which was, 'Stand up for yourself; you deserve to make more money. Don't let people look down on you.'"

■ Contractors 2000 to Nexstar Network

I brought Frank in to teach his seminar, "The Business of Contracting," to members of the Minnesota Plumbing-Heating-Cooling Contractors Association (MNPHCC) in 1991 while I was assistant executive director there.

The seminar was a big hit and many members immediately adopted Frank's flat-rate business model.

At about the same time, Frank's columns for *PM Magazine* caught the attention of a fellow contractor named George Brazil who was doing something in California similar to what Frank was doing in Milwaukee. George contacted Frank and invited him to do seminars out West.

Frank and George were forces of nature individually, but together they were a natural phenomenon. Both were incredibly creative, and both were determined and aligned in their belief in the need to elevate the image and performance of the mechanical contracting profession. Frank and George shared a deep conviction that this *must* happen. This was not just an idea—it was a life's mission for both of them.

The result of this partnership was Contractors 2000, which is now known as Nexstar Network. The rest is history.

The primary purpose of this book, however, was not to tell the story of Nexstar but rather to help you create your future in the same way that Frank and George did. One in which you can live the way you really want and deserve to live as a craftsman in this amazing industry. Because, as we hope you realize by now, you are worth it. ■

ACKNOWLEDGMENTS

Along the way, over the past 25 years, many things have to come together for me to be in a position to write a book. But what was most important was support. I approached the Nexstar board of directors with the idea, knowing that it would take organizational time and resources. They were immediately 100 percent supportive. Special thanks to these amazing members who served on our board during the time the book was written: Arnie Shaw, Marty Cullen, Matt Bergstrom, Jaime DiDomenico, Mark Presgrave, Jeff Belk, Phil Smitherman, Jeff Allen, Chris Corley, Elaine Damschen, and Kevin Wolf. They are extraordinary.

I would like to tell you that the idea of a Nexstar book was mine, but it was not. It was Rachel Whitman's idea, and while she is no longer with Nexstar I would like to thank her for her vision.

Writing is not a chore for me, but writing a full book is not something I had ever attempted. It is very different than writing an article or other business communication. Guiding me along the way was Helena Bouchez of Executive Words, who helped shape the order and kept us on plan. Without her counsel, this book would have remained an idea only.

I would also like to thank the many members and staff who took the time to read an early draft and offer feedback and encouragement: Julian Scadden, Marla Coffin, Greg Niemi, Jim Hamilton, John Conway, Bill Raymond, Brad Martin, John Ward, Gordon Schroll, Scott Nelson, Tom Kelly, and Dan Weltman. They were all very thoughtful and supportive and added content from their own rich experiences.

Finally, to the incredible men and women of Nexstar, who truly serve our members with distinction, giving me time to work on special projects such as this one. Nexstar is amazing because of the people, members, and staff who serve the organization and share their experiences. Without them, there would have been no book to write. ∎

ABOUT THE AUTHOR

J ACK TESTER was the first employee of Nexstar, hired by Frank Blau Jr. and the founding board of directors to bring the vision of the organization to life. During his initial six-year tenure, Nexstar grew from a fledgling one-man shop to a respected national organization with 270 members. Jack departed Nexstar to manage a large national plumbing, HVAC, and electrical service company but rejoined in 2006 as a business coach and coaching manager. He has served as CEO of Nexstar since 2011.

Jack's 360-degree perspective derives not only from having run a one-truck company and a more than $500 million service company, but also from allowing hundreds of member companies to stand on his shoulders so they could see farther and reach higher. His unique point of view is shared throughout the pages of this book.

Currently, Jack and his wife of more than 30 years, Barbara, reside in Newport, Minnesota. They have two adult children, Lauren and Brent, and he is very proud of them. Jack is an avid out-doorsman who spends his free time flushing grouse behind his two springer spaniels or wading in a trout stream. He also curses at the TV on fall Sundays, thanks to a lifelong addic-tion to the Minnesota Vikings. ▨